AF338261

"Nass Cannon treats the reader with his profound humility, grace, and passion for living a life of giving. As a physician he gives voice and meaning to his call for health-care professionals to embrace *caritas*, 'a spirit of seeking the well-being of the other person,' to return tenderheartedness to our bureaucratic and balkanized health-care system. Essential reading for those choosing a career as a health professional."

—**Max Michael**, professor and dean
emeritus, UAB School of Public Health

"This book provides a beautiful spiritual memoir of a contemplative man who found exceptional guidance, growth, and brotherhood in the writings of Thomas Merton. In compiling their father's writings, Nass Cannon's children have honored his life and given us glimpses of the way in which he lived. His legacy continues to flourish in their adult lives, as well as in the lives of all whom Cannon touched in his own embodiment of the Broken Healer."

—**Doris Greiner**, associate professor
emerita, University of Virginia

"Whether reflecting on his own experience as compassionate physician and wounded healer or providing incisive commentary on key aspects of the contemplative, prophetic spirituality of Thomas Merton, the essays of Nass Cannon compiled in this volume are sources of profound insight and challenging inspiration. Deep gratitude is due to his children Clare, John, and Bryant for making these writings of a wise, faithful contemporary Christian disciple and role model available to the rest of us."

—**Patrick F. O'Connell**, editor, *The Merton Seasonal*

IN SEARCH OF THE HEALING SPIRIT

In Search of the Healing Spirit

Nass Cannon Jr.

Edited by
Clare E. B. Cannon,
Bryant Cannon,
and John Cannon

RESOURCE *Publications* · Eugene, Oregon

IN SEARCH OF THE HEALING SPIRIT

Resource Publications
An Imprint of Wipf and Stock Publishers
199 W. 8th Ave., Suite 3
Eugene, OR 97401

www.wipfandstock.com

PAPERBACK ISBN: 978-1-6667-5553-4
HARDCOVER ISBN: 978-1-6667-5554-1
EBOOK ISBN: 978-1-6667-5555-8

06/09/23

For our family

"For now we see in a mirror dimly, but then face to face;
now I know in part, but then I will know fully
just as I also have been fully known.
But now faith, hope, love, abide these three;
but the greatest of these is love."

—1 Corinthians 13:12–13

Contents

Foreword by John Cannon | ix

Acknowledgments | xvii

Introduction by Bryant Cannon | xix

1   The Broken Healer | 1

2   A Quest for Health | 8

3   Concupiscence or Caritas: A Choice of Guiding Spirits | 23

4   The Tears of Things: A Meditation on Grief | 31

5   No Mirror, No Light—Just This! Thomas Merton's Discovery of Global Wisdom | 38

6   Attending to the Presence of God: Thomas Merton and *le Point Vierge* | 54

7   A Certain Victory: Thomas Merton and the Journey of Personhood | 64

8   Thomas Merton and St. John of the Cross: Lives on Fire | 74

9   Stand on Your Own Feet! Thomas Merton and the Monk without Vows or Walls | 85

10   A Path to Peace: Thomas Merton, Final Integration, and Us | 105

11   The Road to Joy: A Circle Dance of Love, Thomas Merton, and the Pursuit of the True Self | 108

Contents

12 A Stranger No More | 119

13 Reflections: Grow Foolish in Love | 129

Afterword by Clare E. B. Cannon | 133
Bibliography | 139

Foreword

Mary struggled with mental illness and lived under a bridge. A kind and genuine black woman in her sixties, she had met Dad while begging at St. Paul's Cathedral in Birmingham, Alabama, where he regularly attended daily Mass at noon. Dad became friends with Mary, and would sometimes talk to her after Mass. Eventually, he even sponsored her lodging at the local YWCA and helped provide for some of her needs. He did all this quietly; even our family didn't know about it.

When Dad was diagnosed with terminal cancer in November 2017, I was living in a Carmelite monastery in formation to be a priest. I was given permission to help care for him while he was dying. Mary's birthday was coming up in early January 2018, and Dad made every effort to schedule all of his commitments during this day so that he could do something special to celebrate her birthday. Although he was incredibly sick and had many other obligations that day, he arranged doctor appointments and the entire day around celebrating her birthday. I had the privilege of joining them.

We didn't know it at the time, but it would be one of his last days of consciousness. He was in the waning days of battling cancer. Although Dad could barely walk and felt extremely sick, we took Mary to lunch and then grocery shopping. Shortly after we arrived at the grocery store, Dad became violently ill from the cancer and chemotherapy medicine. He asked me to shop with her and "get her anything she wanted." I walked with Mary around the store, and she occasionally put items in the basket. Then we checked out and waited for Dad to emerge from the bathroom.

By the time he came out of the bathroom, he looked at the cart half-full of groceries and said in an almost inaudible voice, "That's not enough." Despite Mary's objections, he took her shopping around the store a second time. Barely able to walk, talk, and on the verge of dying, he did another lap with her around the store to get her anything she might need and more. He hunched over the cart, using it as a sort of walker to prop up his failing body. He grabbed a small cake, then balloons, and even flowers for Mary. No one celebrated Mary's birthday, so Dad wanted to make it special for her. He knew it would be the last time he could do something to make her feel special, feel loved.

This lunch and shopping trip with Mary was, quite possibly, the most complete and beautiful act of charity I'd ever witnessed in my life. Despite having nothing left and being in agony, he poured out kindness and generosity to someone who could never pay him back. It turned out to be Dad's last day before being checked into a palliative care clinic, where he would die a week later.

Professionally, Dr. Nass Cannon was an internal medicine and infectious disease physician. For over forty years, he worked at Cooper Green Hospital in Birmingham, Alabama—a hospital dedicated to serving the poor and those without insurance. He cared deeply for the poor, those who suffered, and especially the plight of the homeless. He developed a reputation in the poor community of Birmingham as a compassionate and good doctor.

Once, after getting in trouble and needing to pay off hours of community service at a soup kitchen, I was assigned to scrub pots and pans that seemed to stretch from the floor to the sky. When the head of the soup kitchen saw my last name on the paperwork, she came up to me asking, "You ain't Doctor Cannon's son, are you?"

Sheepishly I replied, "Yes?"

Quickly she replied, "Oh no. You ain't cleaning those pans. Come on in the kitchen and help us with the food. Yo daddy was the best doctor I eva had!"

Encounters like this happened with some consistency. As kids, workers at the movies would try to sneak us into the theater when they saw my dad. Other people would light up when they saw him on the street. He treated his patients not just as problems to be solved but truly as humans in search of healing. He knew that only part of healing was medical. Much of it was emotional, mental, and spiritual. To amplify his work of healing, he allowed God to work through him and touch people's lives. I think this is why so many of his patients loved him and found so much healing through him. They encountered not just a doctor, but someone who radiated the love and mercy of God, the Divine Physician.

His love for his patients and community was not detached from the kindness and love for his family. Rather, he prioritized family, which I think empowered him to impact others in his work and community. Dad took off work every Friday afternoon when we were young. He would take us to all sorts of places—to the botanical gardens for walks, fishing, to Mass, museums, the arcade, parks, and so many other places and activities. He spent countless nights helping us with homework, attending our sporting events, and just being available whenever we needed him.

He seemed to always put our needs and wants first. In fact, we *rarely* knew what he wanted, and it seemed his only real needs were to attend Mass every day and have some time for prayer. These were non-negotiables for him, but, in pretty much everything else, he was available to serve the needs of the present moment, especially with his family, patients, and those whom he encountered in the ordinary events of life. He loved having the family all together and took time for two family trips every year to visit his mother and family in North Carolina, where he was born and raised.

His love also shone in the simple, little things—a frequent and kind smile, patient listening, helping others in hidden ways, and praying for his family and those in need. These small daily acts of love, accumulated over a lifetime, carry incredible weight. Since his death, I have been struck by how he was almost universally loved. Nearly everyone who came in contact with him remembers some kindness he showed them.

To share just one of many examples of how his kindness radiated outward: My mom had a rug cleaned a few years after Dad's death. The owner of the store said it would take weeks to get it back. After the man saw in his system that she was married to Dad, he said, "Wait, Nass Cannon was your husband? He was a great man. I will have this ready for you tomorrow." Dad only met this man a few times in the routine context of having an occasional rug cleaned. But my father somehow made an impression and difference in this man's life—so much so, that many years later, the man's memories of Dad transcended his role as a customer and reflected the powerful impact Dad had through mere incidental contact. But, perhaps that's the point. For Dad, no contacts were incidental.

Unsurprisingly, he was especially beloved by his friends, many of whom were Catholic priests. After Dad died, one of these priest friends preached a homily almost entirely dedicated to sharing about my dad's example of a holy life, even saying, "Dr. Cannon was the most present person I've ever known. When you spoke to him, his entire person was there listening to you and caring for you." Similarly, one of the older, wiser Carmelite friars I lived with for a time, said, "Your father was one of the few truly great men I've ever known."

Dad's love of others was profoundly evident in his family and his care of patients, but it was not limited to this. One of his favorite Christmas gifts to us was to sponsor an orphaned child in India in our name. Over the years, he sponsored at least fourteen children—paying for their schooling, food, and healthcare—wanting to give them a better chance in life and show them love. Much of his charity was behind the scenes, quietly helping the homeless or those in need whenever they came to him. In fact, he almost never turned down beggars on the street or those who showed up at our door asking if they could do some work for pay.

Anyone who knew Nass Cannon—Dad to us, Dr. Cannon to many, family or friend to more—recognized immediately his humility, kindness, patience, gentleness, and so many other virtues. What was his secret?

More than anything else, he was a Christian. During his twenties, for a time, he fell away from church and faith but eventually found his way back and embarked on a four decade journey cultivating a profound relationship with God. He was a deeply and resolutely faithful Catholic. He was given the gift of an abiding faith in Christ and he nourished this faith through attending Mass—every day—for forty years. He loved Mary, the mother of Jesus, and came to know her especially as "Mary, the Mother of God." He said she looked over our family while we were growing up. Dad had a relationship with the saints and theologian and scholar Thomas Merton, eventually becoming a prayerful scholar on Merton's life and writings. The collection of writings that follow exemplify this reflective scholarship.

He was deeply in love with the Eucharist, with holy communion. Receiving the body of Christ at Mass each day was his spiritual nourishment that abundantly overflowed to all aspects of his life. This relationship deepened over the years. He went to confession every week. Confessing his sins to the priest was, for him, a way of cleansing his soul and opening himself to the mercy of God. However, these are not things he spoke of openly. As one family member told me, "His faith was so sublime, he rarely spoke of it."

During Dad's last days, I had the great blessing of taking him to Mass in the morning and being with him at a sacred time in sacred places. The morning after celebrating Mary's birthday, I came into his room to wake him up as he was late getting out of bed. Something was different that morning, and he couldn't move his legs to get out of bed. He became slightly frustrated with not being able to get ready for Mass. I told him, "It's OK Dad, we don't have to go to Mass today. We can stay here and rest."

With a look of determination, he told me to dress him and help him up. I quickly dressed him and helped him up from bed, and almost carried him down the stairs and into the car that icy January morning. We eventually made it into Mass and sat in the back. He was in such pain, he could barely lift his head and could not walk up to receive communion. He told me, "Can you ask the minister to bring me communion here?"

I felt a little uncomfortable with this because it was a large church and it would be awkward for the minister to walk all the way back to give him communion. In fact, in my thousands of masses I don't think I'd ever seen a priest walk all the way to the back to give one person communion. Nonetheless, I asked the priest to come back and give my dad communion. The priest walked the length of a football field to the back of the church and gave Dad communion. Despite nearly every obstacle imaginable, Dad would not be separated from the Eucharist. He needed Christ in the Eucharist like he needed life itself. At the end of Mass, Dad asked for the priest to hear his confession. The priest, who knew Dad, knelt beside him and listened to his confession. Although I couldn't hear anything, I watched this through the glass church doors as I stood in the cold morning. When he was finished, the priest gave him absolution and a blessing as tears streamed down Dad's face. I carried him back to the car. Within hours his body was shutting down and we rushed him to a palliative care center, which had an open bed. By the next day, he was unconscious and died a week later.

I witnessed many acts of my father's faith, deep prayer, love, and mercy toward others. Together they could fill a book of their own. I believe Dad arrived at the doorstep of the infinite love of Christ by this last week of his life. I imagine this love was only intensified by the profound suffering he endured during his final months and especially the last agonizing week in palliative care— immense pain throughout his body while he was no longer able to eat or drink.

Nass Cannon's life was rooted in Christ and a fidelity to the Catholic Church. He was spiritually nourished by the sacraments of holy communion and confession as well as deep prayer throughout the day. This was his lifeblood. Truly it was Christ living in him that brought so much love through his life. Dad's life pointed to Jesus. I pray that we all have the grace and humility to imitate this profound and sublime love. And I pray that his faith, hope, and love have been fulfilled as he gazes forever upon the face of God.

Along with my mom (and Nass Cannon's wife of forty-five years), Gail Barber, my brother, Bryant, and sister, Clare, it's a blessing to share some of the writings of our beloved father, friend, and hero, Nass Cannon. May these writings be encouraging, nourishing, and fruitful for all who encounter my father through them.

John Cannon
March 2023
Washington, DC

Acknowledgments

We would like to thank our mother, Gail Barber, and loved ones for supporting and encouraging us to develop this book in honor of our father's legacy. We are especially grateful for the support of our spouses, children, aunts, uncles, cousins, family, and close friends, in developing this work.

Introduction

Our late father, Dr. Nass Cannon Jr. (MD), was born in 1943 as the youngest of four children to immigrant Lebanese parents who ran a small town department store in Farmville, North Carolina. He emerged from North Carolina tobacco country searching for his place in the world and cast his sights further afield. First to the University of Notre Dame, before returning to North Carolina for medical school at UNC-Chapel Hill, before venturing deeper into the South, where he landed in Birmingham, Alabama, as the city staggered out of the 1960s civil rights movement and into the economic dislocation of the 1970s. Against this backdrop, as the region's steel industry shuttered, the urban core hollowed out, and income inequality surged, Dr. Cannon rose to become clinical professor of medicine at the University of Alabama at Birmingham Medical School. But as a devout Catholic, who spent his life growing in faith and wisdom, he was called toward addressing the plight of the poor to help in their healing. In 1983, Dr. Cannon became a physician at the county hospital recently established to provide healthcare to all, including those unable to afford medical services. At Cooper Green Hospital and Mercy Clinic, he held various positions over four decades, and served a third of that time as its chief of staff. In this role, Dr. Cannon's life was devoted to fighting for healthcare equality and racial dignity based on the belief that healthcare is a right, not a privilege of only those who can afford it. Serving the poor and forgotten was central to his mission, teaching of medical residents, and personal life.

An inquisitive and caring soul, Dr. Cannon questioned the orthodoxy of commercialized healthcare and heeded his call to service as a longtime physician for the indigent poor. His search for spiritually nourishing healing ultimately led to his explorations concerning the theologian and monk Thomas Merton. Dr. Cannon did not see healing and spirituality as independent spheres but as conjoined parts of an individual's overall health. Health and spirituality were intricate components of one's path toward joy. In this way, he ultimately found that Thomas Merton's passion for the fullness of life amid monastic quietudes paved a path worth exploring.

Dr. Cannon and Merton both started their deepest spiritual journeys in pursuit of their callings from a place of deconstructed bareness. Merton's trials led him to Cistercian Trappists in Kentucky, where his brokenness served as fuel for the fire of his spiritual ardor and prolific theological explorations. Dr. Cannon, in his own way, confronted the notional idea of physician as exemplar and probed how a healer's healing derived its greatest power from engaging with our shared human frailties. Dr. Cannon, through his essays "The Broken Healer," "A Quest for Health," and "Concupiscence or Caritas" challenged the relationship between healer, patient, and the institutionalizing forces of a desensitized healthcare industry amid unfettered capitalism's more broadly corrosive effects on society. Dr. Cannon's early search for the healing spirit is bookended with his revelation in "The Tears of Things" that binding oneself to a deep contemplative practice may sublimate rancorous grief and provide a means for processing grief, joy, and the love that lies between.

Dr. Cannon used Merton's insights as a contemplative mirror to examine his own spiritual journey as a broken healer ("No Mirror, No Light—Just This!"), authenticity ("Attending to the Presence of God"), actualization of one's full self through passionate loving engagement with the world ("Thomas Merton and the Journey of Personhood" and "Thomas Merton and St. John of the Cross: Lives on Fire"), the integration of monastic spiritual balance with lay professions ("Stand on Your Own Feet! Thomas Merton and the Monk without Vows or Walls"), before finally taking us toward joyful love ("A Path to Peace," "The Road to Joy," "A Stranger No More," and "Grow Foolish in Love").

In this way, Nass Cannon's writings have been organized in this book according to themes that animated his life: health, spirituality, and love. These themes were present and alive in the three most important domains he traversed on his own road toward a joyful life—his call to medicine, his active faith, and in abiding lovingness toward all, especially his family. From the outset of his journey to serve those most in need, Dr. Cannon explored what it means to be broken and called to heal each other, ourselves, and the world. From this position as a broken healer, Dr. Cannon's meditations over the course of his life of service increasingly wrestled with the transformative implications of Merton's theology. This lifelong study of Merton and other souls on fire offers readers in search of the healing spirit a torch to illuminate new areas of healing, spirituality, and love on their own road to joy.

This collection of essays provides an exploration of the routes toward healing and reveals that through our brokenness we encounter godly love, which has the power to heal ourselves, each other, and the world.

Bryant Cannon
March 2023
Berkeley, California

1

The Broken Healer[1]

I AM A PHYSICIAN who views his root identity as one called to heal. Yet, I experience myself as broken, as one admonished by the phrase, "Physician, heal thyself." Perhaps you, too, in your healing ministry, experience yourself as a broken healer. Let us together explore some notions regarding the healer as broken, examine the nature of healing, and consider the relationship of the healer to one healed.

THE HEALER AS BROKEN

More than most, healers—all of us—share in the mortality and brokenness of all. We experience our brokenness as physical, mental, and spiritual. We are not immune to the wear and tear of too many sleepless nights, lack of exercise, ulcers, heart diseases, cancer, strokes—the lot of man and his human condition. In our care for our patients, we ponder their decline and see ourselves, as though we were looking into a mirror and watching our own

1. Variations of this chapter have been published in *Educating the Christian Doctor*, 35–42, and *Humane Medicine*, 121–23.

deterioration. We breathe sickness, suffering, death, and dying—we inhale the phenomena like a chain smoker, all the while with a finger on our pulse and a self-reflective mind awaiting our own inevitable collapse. We move through the world of sickness and suffering, not as an observer, remote and detached, but as a participant, one victim among other victims; the days, the nights, become a blur of tormented faces, racked bodies, confused minds—an endless stream of suffering humanity passing by—not so much before us as with us, as together we march toward death.

As we minister unto others, we must not be surprised at our own capacity for betrayal and even evil. As broken healers, we will find in ourselves the darkness that is part of our interior. Rage, sadism, violence, disgust, hatred, rejection, malice, envy, greed, pride, jealousy, lust, rebellion are all part of us. In our encounters, these dark forces often surface, tempting us to injure those we seek to heal. Also, long exposure to suffering creates a numbing effect—an anesthetization of our sensibilities best classified and expressed as indifference. The recognition of these forces in us is an opportunity for humble growth. By acknowledging our weaknesses and seeking forgiveness when appropriate, we find healing as we seek to heal.

Two virtues—not often discussed but direct fruits of our brokenness as healers—are an experience of sorrow and growth in tenderheartedness.

As healers, we experience sorrow in our relationships with others—sorrow in our errors of judgment, sorrow in our limited capabilities, sorrow in our neglect and indifference. We inhabit a world of sorrow, a world deeper than regrets or sadness, a world in touch with the aches and pains of the human heart. This pain-filled world is more than just a reaction—"I am sorry": It is deeper than that. Sorrow is a property of love, when there is nothing it can do to change the suffering of the other person, other than suffer with them. Sorrow presupposes care, concern, and love. A measure of our love is a measure of our sorrow.

Tenderheartedness is more than sympathy. A virtue, opposed to indifference, it is an interior stance—an attitude more easily recognized by another person than by oneself. It involves having tender feelings, but tenderheartedness is more than just feelings. There are times when storms of anger, revulsion, frustration, and even rage arise in our encounters. Tenderheartedness relates to the will to treat others as you would have them treat you—no matter what the circumstances. It is to have a human heart, a will to encounter a human person, not a disease or a process. It is the constant struggle not to let our beliefs, prejudices, and feelings create barriers in our encounters. Tenderheartedness must not be misconstrued as the evasion of a hard decision or even softness in the face of a necessary confrontation; the denial of emotion; or retreat before the truth of physical, mental, or spiritual realities. Rather, it is an interior stance of openness, of receptivity: an I-wish-you-well attitude. It regards you as a friend, and its communications are I-wish-to-help-you. A measure of the depth of our personal experience of our brokenness, a tender heart radiates kindness, patience, and compassion.

Brokenness is a precondition for healing. This power to heal, an incomprehensible mystery, the Way of Divine Love, can be experienced, even though not understood. When God says, "What do you want?" we say, "To be healed, to be reconciled." We expose our brokenness. Touched by *his* healing power, we experience the healing of our own bodies, minds, and souls. But, we also discover, he says, "Go and do likewise." In the mutual dependence of the healing encounter, we learn that he heals us as we consent to heal others. We are reconciled as we reconcile. We discover that our brokenness is a precondition for healing.[2] Our search for health of mind, body, and soul through the medium of God's power to heal becomes the source of healing for others—our brokenness conjoined to his. Exploding then from the very depths of our brokenness comes the power to heal. As we assent to heal one another, to care for one another, God assents to heal us, to care for us, so that, in the process of healing, we find healing—because that is the medium through which he chooses to encounter us.

2. Nouwen, *Wounded Healer*, 1–3.

THE NATURE OF HEALING

The essence of healing is not the alleviation of suffering (although that is an important element), but reconciliation. Genuine healing is not simply a repair process, a replacement of spare organs, or the eradication of an infectious illness. Genuine healing transcends the repairing process to include deep integration of body, mind, and spirit.

Healing involves a reconciliation of the body as made subject to mind, and mind made subject to spirit, and spirit made subject to the Spirit of God. This reconciliation is an integration, a harmony, a tendency toward wholeness, a subjection of priorities—body to mind, mind to spirit. Our bodies could be put in the service of our minds, harnessed to a spirit of power, of domination: a Herculean body could be put in the service of an ascetic and disciplined mind, and thereby put into service of this world. Alternatively, a disciplined body could be harnessed to an orderly mind, put in the service of the "suffering servant,"[3] characterized by love, gentleness, service, justice, and peace in relationships.

There are priorities in healing. God's priorities may not be ours. Perhaps, his highest priority is the healing of the soul, then the mind, then the body. The phenomenon of human suffering is a mystery and will remain so. But sometimes it seems that the body is allowed to suffer and the mind assaulted for the sake of building up spirit-generating virtues. Our allocation of resources reverses these priorities. Most of our attention is directed toward the body, little to the mind, and virtually none to the spirit.

Isaiah's account of the suffering servant[4] reveals, in mystery, the heart of all healing. In his account, healing arises from a suffering servant whose stripes and brokenness generate healing. We, as healers, are invited to share in the brokenness of the suffering servant; we are invited to explore our own brokenness, to join it to his, and share, too, in his power to heal. Healthcare, as a composite of care providers with specialized knowledge, medications,

3. Isa 53:4–6.
4. Isa 53:4–6.

technology, and procedures, ensues in a profound encounter if permeated by *the spirit of the suffering servant.*

THE HEALER'S RELATIONSHIP TO OTHERS

We, as healers, in our relationship with the suffering other, experience our human insecurity. We experience our limitations, the fragility of our lives, our essential oneness with the suffering other person. This experience may be characterized by the statement "there but for the grace of God go I." We may penetrate the suffering of the other in empathetic degrees. First, through knowledge of the suffering other, we acquire a conscious awareness of the content of their suffering. Through our ongoing relationship, we immerse ourselves in the other's suffering through empathetic understanding. As our intimacy progresses, we can progress to "feeling" the other's pain. This pain and suffering are like that which occur in a loving family when a child is sick or brother ill. There is a final degree of involvement, very rare and unique, that belongs to the mystical realm. Imitators of the Suffering Servant—Saint Francis of Assisi, Saint Theresa (the Little Flower), Padre Pio—voluntarily assent to suffer for others.[5] Somehow the vitality of their voluntary suffering showers spiritual, mental, and even physical healing on others, even though those individuals may be unknown to them personally. Their suffering manifests the concept of a mystical union whereby all of us are somehow tied to one another and affect one another, both living and dead, through the mystery of our forming one body in human community. Our healing relationships with others are concrete (physical), mental, emotional, and spiritual. We concretely touch and provide services that are physical; we intellectually and mentally engage the content of their suffering and devise plans of therapy and solutions to their problems. We engage them emotionally as well. We relate spiritually to them through our prayers, our dialogue, our worship.

5. Clarke, *St. Thérèse of Lisieux*, 1–3.

COMMUNITY

Another important aspect of our healing relationships is the necessity of community. The phenomenon of healing is not an individual event, not only in the obvious sense of support personnel, nurses, secretaries, chaplains, doctors, janitors, and therapists—all of those individuals who make a healing encounter possible—but also in the sense that the power to heal resides in the community. It is not the property of doctors or nurses or account managers. For that matter, it is no one's property. It is a gift that dwells collectively in the community and can manifest itself most forcefully when the whole community mobilizes itself to care for the suffering other. So, it is a communal event in the direct, supportive, healing relationships of family and friends and in the invisible relationships of prayer and church services. We broken healers must then pay attention to one another, learn to listen to one another, have respect for one another's unique healing gifts, affirm them, develop them, and allow them expression in our communal ministry.

In our communal healing ministry, we should come to listen reverently to the testimony, the witness of the suffering other. We must receive the communications of our patients as more than factual exchanges. We must listen deeply for the faint sounds of the divine spark writing us a letter of love in the concrete humanness of our sufferers as we hear the disclosure of their story, of who and why they are, of the pains and hurts of being them. As we grow in our regard for suffering others, we may come to feel for them as though they were our sons or daughters, our brothers or sisters. This tender regard can progress to experiencing them as our very other selves. But, in this experience, we see that others' suffering is their own and not ours, and that their relationships, personal history, traditions, and so on, are distinctly theirs and not ours. Yet somehow, we complement and complete each other; somehow, we are one.

And so, the whole communal aspect of the healing process should be approached just so—as a big family. This brother with cancer, this one with heart problems, this sister with leukemia, this little brother with AIDS.

Two young men with AIDS died recently. During their long, difficult struggle, they came to know the heart of rejection. They lived at the center of isolation. They were perceived as biological founts of contagion, viewed with suspicion, distrust, contempt, and hatred. Never have I encountered such despair as gripped these young men. The last one to die was fecal incontinent. His mother cared for him. Her family and other children shunned them. They had no money, no food, no gas. Their washing machine broke!

AND WHERE WAS I?

The second one, a Catholic, was discharged from the hospital and died at home shortly afterward without even the spiritual consolation of his church!

And where was I?

An eighty-five-year-old man who provided care for his Alzheimer's-stricken wife, as well as caring for a disabled in-law, fell and broke his ribs; he was told that he could not drive again. Faced with the impossible situation of caring for two disabled people and not able even to care for himself, he despairingly took a rifle and shot his wife, his in-law, and himself.

And where was I?

Let us today answer that question. Let us commit ourselves to a new beginning—let us form ourselves into a community of prayer, love, compassion, and tender concern for one another.

Let us become a humane people concerned about the least among us. Let us become a humane society seeking the common good. Let us become a humane world espousing the survival, nurturing, unity, and needs of all humanity.

2

A Quest for Health[1]

This quest for health will examine the nature of health and healing and the formation of the care provider, and reflect on the meaning of caring and the relationships of care provider to care recipient in a communal context.

HEALING THE HUMAN HEART

The Wounded Patient

Often, we do not take time to listen to the stories of the wounded who seek our ministering touch. Knowing their story forces us to approach them as persons who require our time and humanity rather than our objective, impersonal acts of therapy.[2]

Recently, an old lady exposed her wounds. Shuffling to steady her gait, the fat lady leaned on her cane, swung onto the examining table, fixed her brown eyes on me, and said, "I have come to get a blood test." I assumed she wanted a serum cholesterol test.

1. Originally published in *Caring from the Heart*, 28–44.

2. Greiner and Cannon, "I Sent Myself a Card Today," 115.

Impatient with my musing, she blurted, "I want a blood test for the virus." Startled, I focused on the elderly woman who wore a loose blouse, pants, and balanced a very large abdomen that hung almost to her knees. With every movement, arthritic pain shot through dark eyes, with dilated pupils, lost in a sea of flesh. The woman snapped, "I want the AIDS test." More curious, I asked her age. "Eighty," she replied. I shyly asked why she wanted an AIDS test. She related her story.

> I live alone in a project apartment. Three weeks ago, I had a birthday. My children came to my house, brought a cake and food. People who live near me came. Some I did not know so well but have seen. After the party, I took a bath and put on my bed clothes. I went to bed to read. I heard a click in the door like a key turning. Before I could move, a young man jumped on top of me. He beat me on the head and arms, cut my lip and tore my clothes. He raped me. I want an AIDS test.

Having dealt with the reason for her visit, she cried. Violated in body, mind, soul, she sat like a lump of dough reliving the imprint of the semi-stranger who violently stamped her life with the physical, emotional, and spiritual reality of his rape. Twice since then she returned for unrelated complaints. At each visit she told the events of her rape as though the retelling would make it go away. The man continues to live nearby. Although she changed the apartment lock, food, clothing, and money disappear. She sleeps with a pistol waiting for him to return. The assault of the rapist fractures her emotions and wounds her soul. Bruised in body, mind, and spirit, she possesses memories of the event that have become a preoccupation. Although her body regains its daily rhythm, the event is stamped in her memory and colors her emotions with anger, resentment, and alienation. From the encounter, I relearn the essential elements of compassionate caring—listening, identifying, empathizing. Listening to her story opens me to identify and empathize with her suffering, allowing a stranger to become an acquaintance. Her story transforms her from client to person and awakens my compassion as I empathize with this victim of a neighbor.

The Broken Healer

We care-providers-as-healers share in the mortality and brokenness of those we encounter. A few years ago, my brother had abdominal pain. His evaluation revealed gall stones, a duodenal ulcer, and major occlusion of a coronary artery. He received bypass surgery, blood transfusions, and returned to work. Several years later, his physician, evaluating fatigue, diagnosed chronic hepatitis caused by the blood transfusions. He subsequently bled from distended veins, necessitating a special shunt procedure. His other illnesses included a bladder tumor, for which he had surgery and chemotherapy, and diabetes mellitus, which required insulin.

In our care of such as my brother, we ponder a patient's decline and see ourselves as though we were looking into a mirror and watching our own deterioration. We breathe sickness and suffering, death and dying, with a finger on our pulse and a self-reflective mind awaiting our own inevitable collapse. Recently I saw a middle-aged woman whom I will call Sue,[3] with anxiety attacks and ischemic heart disease, or a hardening of the arteries. Sue related that eight months previously her husband and daughter had an automobile accident which killed her daughter and left her husband permanently bed bound. She adopted her daughter's only child, who does not hear or speak, and provides care for her husband. Sue voices frustration, weariness, and anger and expresses guilt for her occasional desire to abandon them. Because of recent robberies in her neighborhood, she cannot sleep, and constantly worries about becoming disabled.

We move through this world of sickness and suffering, not as observers, remote and detached, but as participants. I recall an early morning admission during my medical internship when I angrily stood over a male alcoholic who was vomiting on me.

---

3. Names and identifying characteristics of the patients referred to in this chapter have been changed to protect their privacy.

While I pinched his chest to wake him, I shouted epithets for his self-inflicted injury that kept me from my sleep.

I will never forget the first patient we admitted to our hospital with AIDS at the beginning of the epidemic in the 1980s. Although our team perceived itself to be compassionate care providers, we were smug, intolerant, and fearful about AIDS. We resented the demanding mother who insisted that we provide her son the care and dignity that he deserved. Mother and son exposed our brokenness, forcing us to examine our attitudes and prejudices, and acknowledge our fear. During his lengthy hospitalization, they wore at our consciences and transformed our perceptions from seeing a host with virus to a person with illness. They penetrated our psychic quarantine and opened us to compassionate caring.

Two other fruitful benefits of our brokenness as healers include the experience of sorrow and growth in tenderheartedness. As healers, we experience sorrow in our relationships with others—sorrow in our errors of judgement, sorrow in our neglect and indifference. We inhabit a world of sorrow, a world deeper than regrets or sadness, a world in touch with the aches and pains of the human heart. Sorrow reflects a property of love as we suffer with them, realizing that nothing we do can change their suffering. Presupposing care and compassion, sorrow measures the depth of our love.

Tenderheartedness—a virtue opposed to indifference—relates to an interior tenderness, but tenderheartedness transcends feelings or sympathy. Storms of anger, revulsion, frustration and even rage may arise in our encounters. Tenderheartedness indicates the will to treat others as you would have them treat you, and to encounter a human person, not a disease or a process. It pertains to the constant struggle not to let our beliefs, prejudices, and feelings create barriers in our encounters. Tenderheartedness must not be misconstrued as the evasion of a hard decision, softness in the face of a necessary confrontation, the denial of emotion, or retreat before the truth of physical, mental, or spiritual realities. Rather, it communicates an interior stance of openness such as that of a friend. A measure of the realization of our brokenness, a tender heart projects kindness, patience, and compassion.

We discover that our brokenness is a precondition for healing.[4] Our quest for health of mind, body, and soul through the medium of God's power to heal becomes the source of healing for others—our brokenness joined to his. The power to heal explodes from the very depths of our brokenness.[5] As we assent to heal one another, to care for one another, God assents to heal us, to care for us, so that in the process of healing, we find healing.

The Nature of Healing

The essence of healing surpasses the alleviation of suffering to include reconciliation or personal harmony. Genuine healing goes beyond a repair process—a replacement of spare organs or the eradication of an infectious illness. Genuine healing transcends the repairing process to include deep integration of body, mind, and spirit resulting in wholeness, a unity of body-mind-spirit. It reveals a harmony that transcends body or mind or spirit alone.[6] Even in the face of irreversible disease or disability, this harmony manifests itself.

A friend of mine has multiple sclerosis. Over the years I have watched her mental and physical capacity wane as her spiritual capacity soared. She impatiently wishes to peek beyond the veil, to experience a more complete union with God. Unlike my friend, many persons do not acknowledge their spiritual embodiment, the presence of God within them. In our society, and within the healthcare system itself, most of our attention extends to health of the body, little to mind, and least of all to the human spirit.

There is, nonetheless, a recognition of the experience of mystery in human suffering.[7] We may be able to kill pain with drugs,

4. Nouwen, *Wounded Healer*, 1–3.
5. MacNutt, *Power to Heal*, 1–5.
6. Goodloe and Arreola, "Spiritual Health," 221–26.
7. Starck and McGovern, *Hidden Dimension of Illness*, 1–5.

but these same drugs, as wonderful as they are for treatment, do not touch the core of suffering within the person. Suffering calls for a healing that is relational—a suffering servant. We are all healers, or are capable to serve as such, and through exploration of our own brokenness, as a suffering servant, we may serve and heal.

Formation of Healers

As care providers, how do we acquire a merciful heart? In our training we acquire much skill in the technical aspects of caring but little opportunity to reflect on the origin of our desire to care. The stillness of the human heart has incubated both a Mother Teresa and an Adolf Hitler. Consider the community of hardened hearts (e.g., brewing rage, sadism, murder) that gave birth to the Holocaust. Now, contrast that to the community of Mother Teresa birthing mercy in her service to the poor. The human heart can be filled with grace or evil: grow in wisdom and love or folly and sin—a reality that may in time deform our passions (e.g., facilitate our greed, impel us to murder our neighbor). The heart satiated by excesses of materialism, wealth, and power may become hardened to the cry of those who suffer.

Our modern world abounds in such obstacles. In Western society, materialism, gluttony, lust, and greed have become a way of life. Our eating habits accelerate heart disease; we infect each other with deadly diseases; we consume inordinate resources; we build disposable shopping malls while many of the global population starve. We overindulge the appetites of our bodies, fill our minds with illusionary delights, make our hearts prisoners of our passions. We pursue these destructive ends because our hearts serve these attachments.

To soften our hearts as care providers, some consideration should be given to the means of conversion, the process of freeing our hearts from bondage to destructive attachments and toward merciful concern. The means to do this include fasting, compunction, prayer, reconciliation, and a desire for inner healing.

Fasting liberates the body, mind, and heart. The discipline of fasting allows the mind to be open to the suffering cry. Fasting disciplines our bodies, opens our minds for compassionate regard of our suffering neighbor, and softens the heart for compunction.

Compunction, the sorrow we experience for our heart's inordinate attachment to things, or to the love of self, results from the realization of our failure to love God and our neighbor. Fasting exercises our wills; compunction, as a gift of God's mercy, exercises our hearts. Fasting softens the heart; compunction converts the heart to a love of God and neighbor. Compunction allows us to experience God's forgiveness and mercy, thereby freeing us to forgive ourselves and others. Compunction schools and dilates the heart allowing the care provider to be a channel of God's mercy.[8]

Mercy, a fruit of compunction and the most perfect virtue regulating the relationships of people, manifests itself in goodness toward others. Performing the works of mercy transforms a labor of effort and competence into a labor of joyful love (sorely missed by many practitioners). By contrast, care providers with values conflicting with mercy may render harsh treatment and end in the exploitation of others as commodities. As a commodity, the other becomes someone to whom we do things rather than someone to whom we relate; the person disappears, the three-vessel coronary disease remains. Our institutions for healing become mechanistic assembly lines. The formation of a merciful heart depends upon prayer, through which we communicate not only with God, but with ourselves and with our neighbor.[9]

Prayer allows the integrative power of love to propel us in health of body, mind, and soul as we acquire the spiritual resources to be merciful in our relationships with others. For Christians, a reflection on the hidden life of Jesus may give insight into the meaningfulness of our lives. And not just the living of life, but life as prayer. Before his public ministry, Jesus lived an ordinary life as a carpenter's son while remaining in loving communion with God, his Father. Accepting the Christian belief that Jesus was true man

8. Ward, *Sayings of the Desert Fathers*, 30–33.

9. Merton, *Contemplative Prayer*, 3–5.

and true God, his every thought, word, or deed was in communion with his Father and, therefore, prayer. His moments of solitude, when he communicated in secret with his Father, were no more or less prayer than when he worked as a carpenter. Yet he grew in wisdom and grace through the mundane realities of his everyday life. The love in him animated all that he did, and this love, the very substance of God, made God present in his every activity. Enveloping all of his moments as communion and communication with God, the entire life of Jesus signified a living prayer.

As care providers we can transform our lives into living prayer so that our interactions with the suffering become supercharged with the vitality of the presence of God. Fasting and prayer help us to accomplish the spiritual quest of integration, healing ourselves as we become ministers to others.

The process of reconciliation provides for a healing of the divisions within the self, calming our unhealthy obsessions, balancing the pursuits of body, mind, and spirit into a harmony that makes for peace and allows for personal healing.

This harmony, this quest for peace and inner healing, is nourished by a strong desire for health of mind and soul. Modern psychology and psychiatry have significant contributions to make to the healing of the emotions;[10] God's grace works through these and other modalities. We need help, nonetheless, to allow ourselves to be led. The mystery of human freedom calls us to desire, to choose, while the many impediments of our unruly habits and desires often stand in the way. We need the energy that comes from relationships—our relationship with God and with each other.

Care and the Care Provider

The practice of humane caring requires art, science, and virtue. The art includes such elements as communication skills, a bedside manner conducive to healing relationships, intuition, and a

10. Maher and Hunt, "Spirituality Reconsidered," 21–28.

gentle touch which envelopes the science of medicine.[11] Important virtues include compassion, trust, generosity, and integrity, always providing the care participant space, leisure, and opportunity for partnership. Humane medicine must be rooted in our shared humanity; the golden rule providing guidance for equal partnership. The process of caring derives from being both complementary to and refracting the image and likeness of God, which elevates our encounter to one of communion. Communion occurs when the two of us pass beyond words and the tending of the care of the illness, to the mirroring back of the image and likeness of God to one another. While communion may occur in any encounter, it has a special and unique character in the healing relationship.

The purpose of human caring in the context of healing encounters is to facilitate growth in wholeness. Caring is the human mode of being; each person has the capacity to care. But this capacity may lie dormant for a variety of reasons, rendering one unable to care and, in a sense, inhuman. One may be anti-caring, even bestial. Some of the grotesque abuses of children, the elderly, the disadvantaged, stem from a predatory anti-caring disposition mirroring a deep spiritual disorder. Brutality in all its forms may disrupt the tender roots of caring. Abused children may become abusing parents. Care providers brutalized in their training may be less than ideal communicators of care. This realization has profound implications for medical education.[12]

Teaching Caring

Because of the impacts brutality has on caring, particular attention should be paid in medical and other healthcare educational institutions to the attitudes and behavior of faculty and staff which brutalize care providers. A surgical resident, raked over the coals by his department chief for some minor transgressions, may be faced with the choice of spending his time working toward being

11. Cannon, "How Tender Our Wounds," 231–37.
12. Kohn, "Caring Kids," 496–506.

a superior surgeon at his chief's institution or using his time to care for his wife and two children elsewhere. Students may be brutalized by the rigorous and demanding knowledge requirements, competitive examinations, and alienation from faculty and support staff. Their experience may breed a cynical and harsh, self-centered attitude, which may affect their ability to tend to others like family. Much of the tender roots of human caring that led them into a healthcare field in the first place may be uprooted by the brutality occurring in the name of competence. Because students must demonstrate a certain level of proficiency on standardized examinations, preoccupation with a large volume of information consumes most of their waking hours, leaving little time for nurturing human relationships and their connection to the humanities. Because of this, the human development of the student may be delayed or suffer irretrievable damage.

The care we provide our care providers in training is of critical importance to their acquisition of care competence. Tremendous energy has been given to technological competence and procedural skills, but care competence has been largely ignored. Our educational centers should value, research, and teach the art of caring.[13] Above all, they must foster a caring environment where exemplary caring models are visible. This caring environment places a great but noble onus on the shoulders of presidents, deans, and chairpersons in healthcare institutions.

One of the negative pitfalls of education within busy and crisis-oriented healthcare institutions today is care fatigue. While a frequent occurrence often resulting from excessive and unrealistic demands on oneself and others, care fatigue most often goes unrecognized. Signs of care fatigue may be as simple as an expression of the feeling "If I hear one more complaint!" to a shouting match between a patient and a doctor who has been on call the night before. Recognition of these signs, along with provision for breaks and occasional solitude, are important responses to the age-old, but always perennial, "Physician, heal thyself."

13. Thayer-Bacon, "Caring and Its Relationship," 233–40.

Another difficult challenge in the everyday life of many caregivers today is care provider abuse. Provider abuse may range from a ritualistic call repeatedly made at two a.m. to physical injury or psychologically demeaning behavior on the part of the patient or family. A distinction must be made between patient needs and demands; caregivers have not only the responsibility but the right to establish ground rules for the professional relationships that must exist if healing is to take place.

HEALING RELATIONSHIPS

Nature of Relationships

The care provider exists in relationships. Our ability to care for others depends upon establishing and maintaining healing relationships. Relationship involves the process of intertwining of persons so that they grow in communion with one another and, though separate, create a sphere of common identity. To sustain a relationship, space, leisure, and means for interaction must be available, as well as a common ground (physical, emotional, or spiritual) for communication. The intensity of the relationship escalates as one moves from the physical to the emotional and spiritual. Also, the intensity of the relationship depends upon the space, time, and leisure devoted to it. To establish healing relationships with our patients, we must commit the space, time, and leisure that will nurture communion.

Relationships may be expressed creatively or destructively. Creative relationships manifest love, mutual healing, and affirmation and tend toward union. Mature relationships display sacrificial attributes in which another's interest equals, if not exceeds, one's own. Olivia illustrates this attribute to a heroic degree. Olivia has malignant hypertension and has had two strokes, yet she still serves fifty hungry people through her church ministry. Olivia shops, prepares, and serves her daily meal.

Characteristics of destructive relationships include superior/inferior roles, physical, emotional, and spiritual violence, egocentric behavior, and victimization. Destructive relationships involve power assertions and manipulative self-seeking by one party at the expense of the other. A terrifying example of this occurred when Mary stopped to fix a flat tire. Three men feigned assistance, abducted her, and raped her. Locked in the bathroom, Mary escaped by breaking a window and crawling out.

Broken relationships engender hurts and disappointments which inhibit new relationships. Hence, failure in relationship becomes self-sustaining. Abused children may become abusers; children of divorced parents may carry the pain of separation into their own relationships. The communal consequence of broken relationships includes societal fragmentation and dispersal. Poverty in relationships exist in a society rich in material goods. Societal division and strife originate in our impoverished relationships. Broken relationships result in lack of purpose and societal loss of unity and community. Hurt feelings and the memory of past injuries affect the vitality of one's current relationships, and injuries over a lifetime generate a storm of emotions that can explode at any moment.[14] Wanda, suffering severe spousal abuse for twenty years, shot and killed her husband as he walked into their house with his girlfriend.

Love heals relationships, and the formation of multiple loving relationships at differing levels of intimacy—spouse, children, friends, clients, patients—generates healing in the couple, the family, the community, and society. The individual's decision to love initiates healing relationships. The decision to love joins the human will to the Spirit of Love which enables the achievement of God's purpose for the individual, couple, community, and society.[15]

In the context of healing relationships, our quest for health and wholeness requires our personal conversion and repentance by letting go of our destructive ways, forgiving and forgetting, and turning toward the Source of Love.

14. Linn and Linn, *Healing Life's Hurts*, 1–5.

15. Van Breemen, *As Bread That Is Broken*, 8–10.

The Healer's Relationship to Others

We, as healers, in our relationships with the suffering other, may intensify our communion with them. We identify and penetrate their suffering in empathetic degrees. First, through knowledge of their story, we acquire a conscious awareness of the content of their suffering. Through a sustained relationship, we immerse ourselves in the other's suffering through empathetic understanding. As our intimacy progresses, we can feel the other's pain much like we would in a loving family when a child or brother becomes ill. A final degree of involvement very rare and unique belongs to the mystical realm. Imitators of the Suffering Servant such as Saint Francis of Assisi, or Saint Theresa, the Little Flower, voluntarily assent to suffer for others.[16] Through a mystical union whereby all of us connect to one another and affect one another, the vitality of their suffering showers spiritual, mental, and even physical healing upon others, even though those individuals may be unknown to them personally. This mystical union arises through the mystery of our forming one body.

Healing relationships require community because the power to fully heal resides in the community. It is a communal event in the direct, supportive, healing relationships of family and friends, and in the invisible relationships of prayer and ritual. We broken healers must pay attention and listen to one another, have respect for one another's unique healing gifts, affirm them, develop them, and allow their expression.[17]

In our communal ministry, we should come to listen reverently to the testimony, the witness of the suffering other. We must receive the communications of our patients as more than factual exchanges. We must listen deeply for the faint sounds of the divine spark writing us a letter of love, in the concrete humanness of our sufferers as we hear the disclosure of their story, of who and why they are, of the pains and hurts of being them. This tender regard can progress to experiencing them as our other selves, in which

16. Clarke, *St. Thérèse of Lisieux*, 1–3.

17. Dashiff et al., "Physician and Nurse Collaboration," 57–70.

we recognize our very sameness without losing our individuality. And so, the whole communal aspect of the healing process should be approached as a big family.

Faced with the anguish of the suffering person, we must choose our response as a community of concern. We hope for a kind and merciful reaction, but that is not always the case. Sometimes our hearts, harboring indifference or overloaded with our many concerns, drown the cry of those who are suffering. Nonchalant, mechanistic, impersonal care may follow.

FINAL THOUGHTS

In this chapter we have reflected on healing from many perspectives. We listened to the wounded, observed the broken healers, and examined the nature of healing. We proposed means for the formation of care providers and espoused the golden rule as a principle to govern caring relationships. We concluded that healthy relationships facilitate communion with God and neighbor. We suggested that growth in health, characterized by progressive integration of body, mind, and spirit, leads to wholeness and facilitates union with God and neighbor. The Spirit of God as love actualizes health of body, mind, and spirit and union with our neighbors. Love begets both individual integration and communal unity.

Collectively, our quest for health has a communal extension. By our choices we choose either loving actions that bring individual and communal unity or hateful ones that alienate us from our trust of self, neighbor, and God. Do our choices ferment a society that values community, seeking the welfare of the least, rather than a predatory one that victimizes the elderly and exploits the many for the profit of the few? Do our governments pursue policies that promote the general good, or do they espouse those that have a narrow benefit? Can the mission of a corporation simply be the pursuit of profits without regard for the interests of their employees or society?

Similarly, the world community impacts our individual health as we are either nurtured or assailed by the flow of human events. A society dominated by materialistic values, as well as drugs and violence, creates a poisonous atmosphere for the pursuit of health. An alienated community characterized by lawlessness, injustice, and disharmony births violent communal members. The health of the individual and that of the community are mutually dependent. A stable community with life affirming values and an infrastructure for caring births the development of healthy members. The health of a community may be judged by its unity and the pursuit of humanistic and transcendent values such as mercy, peace, justice, and service.

As care providers we are obligated to choose health with all of its ramifications. Our quest for health of body, mind, and soul will have consequences not only for ourselves but also for our loved ones and our community, because the healing of humanity's heart begins with the healing of our own.

Today, let us begin the journey. Let us seek to "harden not our hearts" to the cry of those who suffer and pursue our mission of mercy. Let us obey the faint, whispering echoes rambling in the cavernous recesses of the wounded as well as in our own broken hearts: "Love one another—May they be one."

3

Concupiscence or Caritas

A Choice of Guiding Spirits

OUR HEALTHCARE SYSTEM IS driven by a spirit of concupiscence. It should be animated by a spirit of caritas. To better understand this, I examine concupiscence from the perspective of its nature, origin, and effect on the individual and on society. To provide a context for examining how the healthcare system is in the service of concupiscence, I include health as a product for consumption, a consumer model of healthcare, and the profit motive.

The spirit of caritas will be described and its effects on both the individual and community enumerated, emphasizing implications for the U.S. healthcare system. The spirit of caritas will be distinguished from a philosophy of violent liberation. I will conclude with a consideration of the priorities for allocation of healthcare resources as dependent upon which spirit guides us.

CONCUPISCENCE

In the context of this discussion, concupiscence is the spirit which inflames our individual and collective appetites to fuel insatiable consumption—a broader notion than simply a lustful longing.

This disordered appetite consumes beyond the amount required for merely necessity, security, or leisure. To satisfy this inordinate appetite, we accelerate our consumption of pleasurable things such as food, activities, and the "products" of a healthcare industry.

Saint Augustine, in his *Confessions*, provides insight into the nature of concupiscence.[1] Saint Augustine was a passionate man, ruled in his youth by the spirit of concupiscence (he had several mistresses and an illegitimate son). A man of inordinate desires, he did not find peace until his heart rested in God. From contemplative intuition and existential experience, Saint Augustine observed that the appetites have an infinite capacity and were restless until they rested in the infinite creator of those passions. He teaches us that (1) appetites seek a happiness that cannot be found in finite objects; (2) the spirit of concupiscence inflames the appetites to seek "pleasure" as an end in itself and not as a means to some other good; (3) concupiscence will make the appetites seeking satiety restless with a fixed amount of consumption and drive them toward an ever increasing need to consume; and (4) appetites become increasingly entrapped in matter as they form a habit of inordinate consumption.

The effect of this concupiscent spirit on the individual causes an individualistic attitude referred to as "individualism." When pervasive, the effect of this spirit on society causes the phenomenon of "consumerism," consumption as an end in itself.

The spirit of concupiscence fuels individualism and a competitive attitude, pushing one to seek the satisfaction of excessive desires even at the expense of another's basic needs. This spirit favors choices benefiting the individual over choices benefiting the community, often compelling the individual to be in opposition to the welfare of the community. Individualism should be distinguished from individuality, where real personal rights must be protected yet balanced with community needs.

The unfettered spirit of concupiscence drives the individual increasingly toward a more radical individualistic expression of his appetites, which from a societal perspective would lead eventually

1. Augustine, *Confessions*, 10–12.

to anarchy. The consequence of individualism is to isolate the interest of the individual from the interest of the community so that competition and disunity prevail. As this individualistic attitude prevails in a society, programs requiring broad-based support, such as healthcare for the poor, suffer.

When the spirit of concupiscence fuels inordinate consumerism, where consumption is a means to the pursuit of happiness and misunderstood as happiness itself. Consumerism, the "market mentality," conveys the message that consumption itself equals happiness, which is often symbolized—if not manifested—by the large shopping center.

These large centers, filled with an astounding array of things, may symbolize our interior state—vast, empty spaces filled with things. We are conscious only of the things; we are not in touch with an implicit poverty within us. Our emptiness is perceived only as a deep hunger, a deep craving we try to fill with things, from food to entertainment, from toys to meaningless facts. Our appetites seek a happiness, a satiety that cannot be found in finite objects.

The spirit of concupiscence imbalances the appetite to seek pleasure as an end in itself. Concupiscence will make the appetites seeking satiety partners with a fixed amount of consumption and drive them toward an ever increasing need to consume. Paradoxically, in the midst of what appears to be plenty, our starvation manifests itself as consumption, an insatiable, inexhaustible hunger, an unquenchable thirst—concupiscence.

One effect of consumerism on society is an acceleration in the economic dislocation of its members. In a world of finite resources, consumerism squanders the world's resources, accelerates the division between the haves and have nots, and ensures that fewer and fewer members of a particular society will have enough. Another effect is the formation of destructive habits—a society imprisoned by consumption turns itself into a junkyard. A future effect may be that all things, experiences, and relationships are for consumption and treated as disposable, including humans themselves. Can you imagine a black market for spare body parts? Even now, there are rumors of transplant organs being bought and sold. What nightmares await us? People maintained as organ reservoirs? Genetically engineered children with immune competence bred as donors? The sterilization of whole races to control for overpopulation?

The spirit of concupiscence animates the healthcare industry through consumerism. Healthcare is advertised as a product to be sold to healthcare consumers (they are no longer patients). Providers are businessmen with stock options and market, content, and advertising strategies. The consumer/consumption model for things has driven a shift to a consumer/consumption model for services, products, and facilities in the healthcare industry. This model of health rests upon the assumption that there is something to buy and sell. Often, what is bought and sold is illusory—what may be termed a sense of health, rather than the concrete, often mundane products, facilities, and services available. Of course, health as such is not purchasable, a fact obscured by the advertising illusion of health and happiness from product A, facilities B, and services C.

Fueled by concupiscence and consumerism, the healthcare industry provides us with an ever expanding array of products, services, and facilities to consume. We, as consumers fueled by the same spirit, obligingly consume them. A probable effect of this spirit on the healthcare system would be an ever increasing maldistribution of services, facilities, and products. We cannot provide an infinite number of services, facilities, or products. As we approach the limits of our capacity, we are forced to make choices about the allocation of our resources. The spirit of concupiscence drives us to allocate the majority of our resources to those with the money to pay for them. If fewer members of society consume more of the healthcare resources, less and less healthcare is available for the poor.

Concupiscence drives the healthcare industry toward inordinate profits and lean budgets, the consequence of which may be an economic rationing of healthcare. Gainfully employed individuals with good health habits consume much of the healthcare products. Their consumption ranges from over-the-counter cold remedies to health checks, annual physicals, health maintenance plans, and more. This individual provides the system with profits and costs little to care for. If this person becomes seriously ill with a chronic disabling illness, her ability to provide profits diminishes as she loses her hospitalization benefits and her income. Over the course of a twenty-year disabling illness her cost to the system could be astronomical. Her capacity or a third-party's willingness to pay would be minimal. What profit-oriented medical business would welcome such a profit loser? The poor, even with Medicaid, are obvious profit losers and have not been welcomed in such a system. Many of the elderly with their multi-system illnesses, their fixed incomes, and marginal benefits (increasingly including Medicare) will also be regarded as profit losers. As profits are highest in those who least need healthcare, the profit losers—the poor, the elderly and the chronically ill—may be rationed out. This spirit of concupiscence fans unnecessary duplication, mismatches services to needs, and encourages placebo practices.

A healthcare system as an industry seeking inordinate profits will not provide healthcare for the poor. Paradoxically, it may not even provide healthcare to those who really need it—the sick. For the sick will drain profits, and treating or healing of those who are ill is not the goal of this kind of healthcare system. A consumer model healthcare system with profits as its highest priority may evolve into one providing care for those who can most afford it, least need it, and receive the least benefit from it; for that is where the profit is. Such a system will exclude the poor, the sick, and the elderly. Apart from the questions of morality and ethics, a system driven by a corporate mentality of bottom-line profits will not work in the long-term interest of individuals or society. It provides the individual the illusion of healthcare security without the substance of it. It will disappear, if not the moment one needs it, the moment after one loses one's health and one's job. Such a system accelerates fragmentation of healthcare resources and promotes inequity in access and quality of care.

Concupiscence and consumerism impair our ability to perceive or even to ascertain the true healthcare needs of the poor.

Preoccupied with our own gratification, we not only underestimate their health needs but opt for individualistic national policies which have a detrimental effect upon them. Societal choices favoring individualistic gratification over community well-being are disruptive of national unity, accelerate fragmentation, and ensure decreased expenditure for the poor.

CARITAS

Caritas is a spirit of seeking the well-being of the other person, even when it costs personal sacrifice. As the spirit of concupiscence focuses the individual's gaze on one's self, the spirit of caritas focuses one's gaze on the other. Caritas originates in the spiritual realm, presupposes the morality of "whatever you do to the least of mine," and expresses itself in compassionate concern for the Other whereby one sacrificially gives of one's wealth, one's time, one's energy.

Caritas is a unique mode of relating to the Other. It is distinguishable from philanthropy, altruism, or a philosophy of violent liberation. Caritas maintains the dignity of the Other as a person, whereas the other modes of relating have the danger of making an object of the Other. Any mode of relating to the poor which allows a fusion of their material poverty into a notion of their essential dignity will in the end make objects of them.

The spirit of caritas is nonviolent, non-manipulative, and non-exploitive. It allows the Other to be, not only as one would like him to be but as he is. It does not try to control nor manage the Other. An individual animated by this spirit does not burden the Other with his own values and attitudes. With regard to the poor, caritas takes them as they are, not trying to make anything else out of them—not a social agenda, not a reaction to guilt, not a question of pity—not to validate the myths of our own sense of superiority.

Caritas must also be distinguished from a philosophy of violent liberation which requires aggression to deliver the poor from their poverty. Such a philosophy in waging war against an oppressor may use the poor as a means for advancing a specific cause rather than focusing on them as human beings in material need. Caritas rejects violent means, does no injury to the Other; rather, it prioritizes well-being and attempts to liberate both the oppressor and the oppressed.

A healthcare system animated by a spirit of caritas would be radically different from a healthcare system animated by the spirit of concupiscence. Healthcare providers would have an attitude of ministering to their patients rather than an attitude of profit-making. They would be motivated by a spirit of compassion—empathy and concern would be the basis for their relationships with patients. Cooperative, collaborative, integrative systems of healthcare would characterize their efforts, reducing wasteful duplication, creating an orderly array of primary, secondary, and tertiary care capabilities with ease of access and equity of care. As cooperation, collaboration, and integration characterize caritas, competition, fragmentation, and division characterize a healthcare system based on concupiscence.

SOCIETAL CHOICES

Societal choices regarding allocation of healthcare resources should be considered by inquiring which spirit shall guide us. Concupiscence will drive us to see healthcare as a product for consumption, resulting in a proliferation of services, products and facilities with increasingly fewer individuals having the opportunity to consume them. In a finite world of limited resources, this excessive consumption could be at the expense of some other individual or group. Blinded by the spirit of concupiscence, we would not correctly perceive the true health needs of the poor and therefore make societal policies which may have a detrimental effect upon them. The consequence of these choices may disrupt society, accelerate communal fragmentation, and ensure even less expenditure for the poor.

A healthcare system guided by the spirit of caritas would be an integrative system, a collaborative effort. It would reassert the dignity of the individual and that individual's right to an adequate level of healthcare. Such a healthcare system would have the attribute of a family spirit, a sense of community with the well-being of the most vulnerable, the poorest, as well as the richest. Such an enlightened healthcare system would reflect a societal realization that we must care for the least fortunate, not only for their interests, but also for our very own, realizing that the vitality and strength of a community is no greater than its least well off members.

Healthcare for the poor along with other programs which benefit the poor become not only a question of distributive justice, but also a question of the ability of a house divided to stand. A competitive, divisive house of medicine squanders resources, fragments healthcare, and disenfranchises large segments of our society. Such a divided house will not long endure.

Our individual and national choices concerning which spirit will guide us become not only a choice of altruism, but a choice of whether we become a vital, integrated family whose strength is our own solidarity, peaceful and secure, or a violent, increasingly fragmented society at war among ourselves.

What is required of us is a change of heart, but let us hope not an artificial one. We need to individually and collectively experience a *metanoia*—to have our passions ruled by a spirit of caritas rather than concupiscence.

For our metaphorical heart is a crucible into which our collective destinies along with the welfare of the poor have been poured—a crucible, flame-fired to white heat by two spirits. This is the hour of our testing; this is the hour of our choice. Which spirit shall guide us?

4

The Tears of Things

A Meditation on Grief[1]

WE HAVE HEARD ABOUT loss and death. We have heard very personal stories of anguish and suffering engendered by the loss of loved ones. And it's all too tempting to be like the friends of Job and give rationalities to human suffering that only end up apologizing for God or blaming the victim or saying "only if."

And how to give grief meaning when there is only hurt and darkness, anger and regrets? And how does one human being dare give expression to the grief of another?

So, it is clear to me that I cannot speak to you about grief as detached observer weighing, analyzing, judging, making sense of it all. I can only speak to you as one small griever among many, as another human being who has tasted grief.

I can briefly catalogue my own grief in childhood separation, loss of jobs, loss of health, loss of a first cousin with a brain tumor, loss of a father after surgery, loss of loved ones in Lebanon from inane violence. And most currently I am watching my forty-nine-year-old brother suffer disability and deterioration from a chronic

---

1. This article, written in 1980 shortly after the death of Nass Cannon's father, Nassif Cannon Sr., was distributed informally.

liver disease—the result of a contaminated blood transfusion—and, yesterday, my mother phoned to say she would need colon surgery for the possibility of a malignancy.

I am a physician, and I am broken by my profession. Daily, I breathe sickness and suffering, death and dying. And, daily, I stand at the foot of the sufferer's cross, sometimes with nothing to offer except encouragement and sometimes not even that, simply mirroring back their own despair. Yes, modern medicine has made wonderful progress, and many live who would have died. But the limits of medicine are the limits of mortality, and we are all faced with the realization that we must die. Medicine can alleviate suffering and prolong life and, as most of you are aware, it can also prolong our suffering and contribute to our demise.

When it comes to dying, medicine—like health, wealth, friends, and even family—will fail us. It is inevitable. And though we can provide and receive support, each of us must die alone. And that is one source of our grief. We watch our loved ones separate from us like a boat leaving the shore, and we are left alone.

I think the depth of our grief has something to do with the extent of our attachment and the depth of our love. Great attachment and love make for great grief. Love calls for our immersion in the loved one: so much so that we die with them. And that ache in our hearts caused by their absence results from the rupture of the spiritual, psychological, and physical bonds our shared life of love has created. The painful rupture of these bonds caused by the demise of our loved ones have their effect on memory, imagination, and in the depths of our souls. The reality of our shared love is coded in our memory and stored in our brains and hearts and becomes part of our physical, psychological, and spiritual beingness. Hence the rupture that results from separation is tasted in our minds and souls and even in the longing of our bodies. And because the loved one is coded in us in these three spheres, suffering is inevitable, and time is required to lessen the wounds. If we love, we shall grieve. It is a price we pay for loving, where two become one. And two become one not only in marital relationships but in every loving relationship, to a greater or lesser extent. The notable author C. S. Lewis wrote a book entitled *A Grief Observed*, which is a journal documenting his reactions to his wife's death. Some of his observations have helped me traverse my own grief. As he writes of it,

> No one ever told me that grief felt so like fear. I am not afraid, but the sensation is like being afraid. The same fluttering in the stomach, the same restlessness, the yawning. I keep on swallowing. At other times it feels like being mildly drunk, or concussed. There is a sort of invisible blanket between the world and me. I find it hard to take in what anyone says. Or perhaps, hard to want to take it in. It is so uninteresting. Yet I want the others to be about me. I dread the moments when the house is empty. If only they would talk to one another and not to me.[2]

C. S. Lewis captures the overwhelming intensity and smallness that surges and recedes amid the tides of grief:

> There are moments, most unexpectedly, when something inside me tries to assure me that I don't really mind so much, not so very much, after all. Love is not the whole of a man's life . . . One is ashamed to listen to this voice but it seems for a little to be making out a good case. Then comes a sudden jab of red-hot memory and all this "commonsense" vanishes like an ant in the mouth of a furnace.[3]

And he explores the coldness of grief amid an unmoored faith:

> Meanwhile, where is God? This is one of the most disquieting symptoms. When you are happy, so happy that you have no sense of needing Him, so happy that you are tempted to feel His claims upon you as an interruption, if you remember yourself and turn to Him with gratitude and praise, you will be—or so it feels—welcomed with open arms. But go to Him when your need is desperate, when all other hope is vain, and what do you find: A door slammed in your face and a sound of bolting

2. Lewis, *Grief Observed*, 22.
3. Lewis, *Grief Observed*, 22.

and double bolting on the inside. After that, silence. You may as well turn away. The longer you wait, the more emphatic the silence will become. There are no lights in the windows. It might have been an empty house. Was it ever inhabited? It seemed so once. And that seeming was as strong as this. What can this mean? Why is He so present a commander in our time of prosperity and so very absent a help in time of trouble? . . . The same thing seems to have happened to Christ: "Why hast thou forsaken me?"[4]

And the daggers of love when two, having become one, are left with none.

Did you know, dear, how much you took away with you when you left: you have stripped me even of my past, even of the things we never shared. I was wrong to say the stump was recovering from the pain of the amputation. I was deceived because it has so many ways to hurt me that I discover them one by one.[5]

As indicative of the passages above and as a writer, C. S. Lewis articulated what all of us have felt. But each of us have our own story and feelings of grief, though we have not always named the feelings we have had, nor the stories.

Experiencing feelings is one thing, but handling them is another. One purpose of support groups is to help in this handling of our feelings of loss. I asked my young friend with multiple sclerosis who has experienced many losses in relationships and health to share with me some ideas about how she handled her grief. She said it is universal, it takes time, and a support group of people with similar losses helps. She also thought being a little busy helped, and acting on social opportunities even if you didn't feel like it helped. She experienced loss as an emptiness that never went away completely but was made less when a loss was replaced with something else.

4. Lewis, *Grief Observed*, 24.
5. Lewis, *Grief Observed*, 67–68.

In the context of my own grief, I found a book by Doug Manning, *Don't Take My Grief Away from Me*, very helpful. After discussing the shock of the immediate loss and things one could do, he reviews some of the stages of grief. He describes the stages as shock: you cry and yet do not feel the brokenness is real; testing reality—deep depression, despair, and dependency; reaction stage—react with guilt, anger, hurt, and frustration; recovery—reconstruct your feelings and decide to live again.

Manning suggests not to let anyone take your grief away from you. He suggests a terrible thing has happened to you, and there is no explanation for why it has happened. Are you supposed to feel happy over it? Or thankful? How are you supposed to react? With a great burst of faith? His answer is that you have been hurt deeply, therefore you should feel hurt deeply. You have a thousand whys and you should ask them all. You have a million feelings; feel them all. You have a billion hurts, and you are entitled to them. Give yourself permission to let go and feel what you are feeling. Don't let them, don't let yourself, take your grief away. Grief should be what it is—cutting if sharp and cold if numbing.

People, often well intentioned, may try to take your grief away by saying too many words. For example, defending God by saying, "Our role is not to question why." They also may try to take your grief away by neglect—avoiding the subject or conveying the impression that if grief lingers faith is weak. They may do it by reacting to your stages of grief in an inappropriate way—"You ought not to feel this way." Manning points out that there is no timetable for healing grief. Quick recovery does not mean you did not love nor long recovery that you loved much. Give yourself permission to grieve as long as you need to, and recognize the ordinary need for it. He suggests we stand up to friends and family, saying, "Don't take my grief away from me. I deserve it, and I am going to have it."

Manning gives some general ideas on relating to children who have sustained loss based on the child's age. Under two, he says they do not have any understanding of death and that it is important that they are not forgotten during the chaos of the immediate experience. Children three to five will have a sense of a bad event occurring but not understand death to any degree of depth. To calm their insecurity, they need love. Children six to eight may have more questions. They will grasp the feelings of insecurity and may come to wrong conclusions about their being responsible for the loss. Time, care, and attention with honest answers to their questions are required. Nine- to twelve-year-old children understand the event surprisingly well, but they relate it in their own terms, like the trip they will not be able to take or the project they will not be able to finish. He suggests that we should be with them in their grief and not misinterpret their concerns as selfish preoccupation. Thirteen to sixteen is particularly difficult. Because of the turmoil of this age, it is easy for these children to connect the event with themselves, thus creating guilt. He emphasizes that there are no magic formulas in dealing with children, but love and good ears are major needs and the best medicine. The major things to help them avoid are insecurity, guilt, which can be real or imagined, and rejection.

Manning emphasizes the barriers that prevent a family from dealing with grief as family—not sharing the hurt and pain and not communicating, going on as if nothing has happened. He suggests a family time much like the old Irish wake (perhaps with less or no alcohol) where everyone comes together to talk about the missed loved one. About the recovery from grief, Manning urges us to also give ourselves permission to stop grieving and to keep living life, though its path is uncertain.

There is a certain rhythm to creation and to life. There is a cosmic dance of a spinning earth around a sun, among countless other stars, with innumerable planets, dancing a galactic ballet. One kick of the moon dancing about the earth gives rise to ocean tides. One bellow of the sun, and we are warmed. And our lives are caught up in this cosmic dance. Like the ebb and flow of ocean tides, life flows from the womb to the tomb. Like the change of seasons, life has its moments of winter and spring. And change, and growth, and loss is part of the cosmic dance. And we come together and we part, we say hello and goodbye. Yet in our personal dance there is something about us that gives meaning to the ballet. Our love for one another makes the dance passionate and personal, caring and human, and transcends the ordinariness of our loving dance together so that we "mount on eagle wings and touch the face of God."[6]

We may all come from different faiths and religious traditions, but I think it is appropriate to note that tomorrow is Easter. And in the Christian tradition, Easter is the great sacred day of the good news. Death has been overcome. Christ has risen. And for the Christian, this is the source of his hope and joy, for the risen Christ is the Christian's pledge that all of his earthly separation is only temporary, and that there will come a time of resurrection when all of us will be united and all of us will be family and all of us will love one another.

And so, whatever our religious tradition, we share in the human condition. We share in our losses. We share in our grief. Let us mourn our losses; let us acknowledge our grief. But let us also live in hope and expectation of a new day, a day of wholeness and love, a day of coming home to our world, ourselves, and our loved ones. Let us let go of the anger, the resentment, the hurt, and the pain; let love alone live in us and let us go forth in our love to shine like the sun.

6. Joncas, "On Eagle's Wings."

5

No Mirror, No Light—Just This!

Thomas Merton's Discovery of Global Wisdom

A polished mirror reflects great light;
a broken mirror generates even more
the greatest light arises from no mirror, no light—just this!

WITH SUPERFICIAL COMPREHENSION OF its meaning, I wrote this Zen-like koan thirty years ago. As my mind wrestled with it over the ensuing years, this koan illuminated my understanding of one's spiritual journey. I came to realize that the light of a polished mirror reflects our true self. The light of a broken mirror is generated from our growth in compassion through the very ground of our brokenness. And the great light that arises from "just this" emerges from the depths of our emptiness where there is no light or mirror, just this—God's own "suchness." In this chapter, I will refer to the imagery of this koan in meditating upon Thomas Merton's spiritual writings and his path to global wisdom.

A POLISHED MIRROR REFLECTS GREAT LIGHT

Thomas Merton chose to become a mirror of love through an actualized life. His early developmental meanderings knew a woman's embrace and the intoxication not only of alcohol, but also of youthful passions which fueled his mind to interrogate the meaning of his life. That enquiry led him in his words "from Prades to . . . Oakham . . . to Rome . . . to Columbia . . . to St. Bonaventure to the Cistercian Abbey of the poor men who labor in Gethsemane. That [he] may become the brother of God."[1] Within the monastery, he sought to amputate the old Merton from his newly ordained incarnation as the monastic Fr. Louis. Instead, he discovered that Fr. Louis was an enlightened old Merton who still enjoyed the passionate pursuit of scholarship and writing and the exploration of life's meaning. He came to Gethsemane to lose himself and find God. Instead, Merton found his true self and discovered this self was also the hiding place of the God he sought.

The path to this discovery is a spiritual journey nurtured by an unseen energy to guide and shape us into our own true individuality and the personhood we become through our interactions. Always present in potentiality, it glides beneath the surface of our awareness and participates in our unconscious, urging us to awaken to who we are. In some, like Thomas Merton, it erupts into consciousness, enticing them into a fuller realization and exploration of their true self, translating its potentiality into actuality, becoming the person we are able to fully become. For Merton, this meant becoming a monk who passionately sought the face of the living God. For him as well as for us, this spiritual exploration begins with polishing the mirror of our interior, which is the conscious pursuit of purity of heart, for "happy the pure in heart; they shall see God."[2]

We begin to seek purity of heart in earnest when we awake to the reality that we have a false self whose identity is built upon

1. Merton, *Seven Storey Mountain*, 462.
2. Matt 5:8.

a lie. At its core, this false self sees itself as a god. In *The Silent Life*, Merton writes of this primal lie:

> The inner, basic, metaphysical defilement of fallen man is his profound and illusory conviction that he is a god and that the universe is centered upon him. . . . Yet in our desire to be as gods, a lasting deformity impressed in our nature by original sin—we seek what one might call a relative omnipotence: the power to have everything we want, to enjoy everything we desire, to demand that all our wishes be satisfied and that our will should never be frustrated or opposed. It is a radical falsity which rots our moral life in its very roots because it makes everything we do more or less a lie.[3]

Sin is at the foundation of our false selves and causes us to dedicate our life to something that God does not know. In *New Seeds of Contemplation*, Merton argues, "And to be unknown to God is altogether too much privacy. My false and private self is the one who wants to exist outside the reach of God's will and God's love—outside of reality and outside of life. And such a self cannot help but be an illusion."[4]

Sin causes us to worship our false selves as an idol and estranges us from our true selves. Continuing this point, in *Thomas Merton in Alaska*, Merton observes, "When you think about what happens if our life is really dedicated to something other than God, then we are first of all alienated, and in a certain sense we are worshiping an idol. We are giving our total allegiance to something that is unreal, something artificial that is not the ultimate reality. That again is the meaning of alienation."[5] In addition to alienating us from our true selves, sin, and its effects, strike at the very depths of our personality. It disrupts our orientation to God, which is the foundation of personhood and personality. As Merton reminds us in *No Man Is an Island*,

3. Merton, *Silent Life*, 13–15.

4. Merton, *New Seeds of Contemplation*, 33.

5. Merton, *Thomas Merton in Alaska*, 76.

> Sin strikes at the very depth of our personality. It destroys
> the one reality on which our true character, identity, and
> happiness depend; our fundamental orientation to God.
> We are created to will what God wills, to know what He
> knows, to love what He loves. Sin is the will to do what
> God does not will, to know what He does not know, to
> love what He does not love. Therefore, every sin is a sin
> against truth, a sin against obedience, and against love.[6]

Sin predicates our false selves upon a lie whose roots Merton traces to original sin. This lie insinuates that if we eat the apple of the knowledge of good and evil, we will be like God. However, the knowledge of good and evil is the "will to do what God does not will, to know what He does not know, to love what He does not love."[7] Thus, the lie creates a false self which, in fact, is that which is not like God.

To recover our true selves, we have to acknowledge this lie. Merton observes in his essay "The Recovery of Paradise" in *Zen and the Birds of Appetite*, "Once we find ourselves in the state of 'knowledge of good and evil' we have to accept the fact and understand our position, see it in relation to the innocence for which we were created, which we have lost and which we can recover."[8] We recover our innocence by grace—choosing growth and integration over division and death—by choosing to love rather than to hate, by choosing to create rather than destroy. We polish our interior mirror by following the promptings of the Holy Spirit, our source of grace, our guide, and our destination. By our choice to follow or reject the Spirit, we are either the mirrors of love and life or hate and death.

Thomas Merton chose to become a mirror of love and life. He tells us in *The Seven Story Mountain* of his own journey to escape the lie of his false self. In the silence of a Cistercian monastery, he sought in earnest to live the proclamation of Eph 5:8, "You were darkness once, but now you are light in the Lord; be as children of

---

6. Merton, *No Man Is an Island*, 84.

7. Merton, *No Man Is an Island*, 84.

8. Merton, *Zen and the Birds of Appetite*, 128.

light." He became a prayerful penitent and seeker of grace, which he found to be a constructive and integrative energy. He opened himself to the grace transmitted through the sacraments of the church but also hidden in nature and in one another. In *Contemplation in a World of Action*, Merton writes, "Those infused with grace seek truth—the truth of themselves, and the truth of their lives, and the Truth that is God, realizing that the only source of the spiritual life is the Holy Spirit."[9]

He sought the guidance of that source to recover his true self. He followed the Spirit's inspirations to the core of his being where he awakened to his true identity in Christ. In *The Inner Experience*, Merton tells us,

> But in fact the Resurrection and Ascension of Christ, the New Adam, completely restored human nature to its spiritual condition and made possible the divinization of every man coming into the world. This meant that in each one of us the inner self was now able to be awakened and transformed by the action of the Holy Spirit, and this awakening would not only enable us to discover our true identity "in Christ," but would also make the living and Risen Savior present in us. . . . Each one of us, in some sense, is able to be completely transformed into the likeness of Christ, to become, as he is, divinely human, and thus to share His spiritual authority and charismatic power in the world.[10]

Our true self and identity is a one-of-a-kind mirror of that babe held in Mother Mary's arms. When we come to know our true selves, we, in some degree, have returned to paradise as a new person with a measure of the innocence present before the fall. Merton writes in "The Recovery of Paradise," "This, as we shall see, is what the Fathers called 'purity of heart', and it corresponds to a recovery of the innocence of Adam in Paradise."[11]

9. Merton, *Contemplation in a World of Action*, 271.

10. Merton, *Inner Experience*, 38.

11. Merton, *Zen and the Birds of Appetite*, 131.

Through our fervent pursuit of God, which, in reality, is our response to God's pursuit of us, we arrive at the realization that our identity is hidden in the identity of Christ. Grace enables us to break through our false selves to discover that the true identity of self is a unique and individual expression of our personhood in Christ. This is our true self. With this realization, we have polished our interior mirror which reflects much light. It reflects the light of truth—the truth of who we are, the truth of how we should live, and the *truth of the presence* of God, concretized in our existence. However, this is not the end of our journey but only the preparation needed to make a true spiritual beginning. Merton continues in his essay "The Recovery of Paradise,"

> Purity of heart is not the ultimate end of the monk's striving in the desert. It is only a step towards it. Paradise is not the final goal of the spiritual life. It is, in fact, only a return to the true beginning. It is a fresh start. The monk who has realized in himself purity of heart and has been restored, in some measure, to the innocence lost by Adam, has still not ended his journey. He is only ready to begin.[12]

Our recovered true self is an infant and, like the infant Jesus, must mature. In the spiritual journey, which is the trajectory of life itself, every arrival is the beginning of another departure.

A BROKEN MIRROR GENERATES EVEN MORE

This departure parallels the maturation of Jesus who grew in "wisdom and grace,"[13] which leads to suffering and the cross. The path involves a connatural identification with nature and immersion in the sacraments, themselves, as well as the living sacraments, which are those we encounter—all animated by the Spirit, the source of wisdom and grace. The signature of our growth is an increase in love and compassion. Realizing one's true identity makes one more

12. Merton, *Zen and the Birds of Appetite*, 131.

13. Luke 2:52.

acutely aware of one's humanity, its fragility and brokenness, and one's kinship with others. As we become more aware of the divine spark of love at the center of our being, we become more human, not less. The presence of this love allows us to identify with our brothers and sisters. In *The Wisdom of the Desert*, Merton observes, "Love demands a complete inner transformation—for without this we cannot possibly come to identify ourselves with our brother. We have to become, in some sense, the person we love."[14]

This love, through prayer, also opens us to a deeper level of conscience which manifests God's life in us in which we and God work together for the benefit of our neighbor. In *Thomas Merton in Alaska*, Merton writes, "The deepest level of conscience is beyond both consciousness and moral conscience; it is beyond thinking and self-awareness and decision-making. It is the conscience of God in us, it is where the Holy Spirit operates . . . Prayer is opening up this deepest conscience and consciousness, in which God and I work together."[15] This conscience leads us to join those who labor in the vineyard, those who choose peace over war, equality over inequality, laws that promote unity and justice over those that foster division and greed. We join those who stand with the poor, the disenfranchised, the victims and refugees of society. We build a community which radiates the light of the truth of the redeemed human condition and the proper relationships of men governed justly.

Our growth in wisdom and grace propels us to grow in Christ's compassion, whose essence centers on the reality of the Word becoming flesh, that man may become divine. This compassion for ourselves and neighbors urges us to desire what he desires, that we all may be joined to his divinity. The path to that quest leads through the heart of our own brokenness and allows us to identify with the brokenness of others. We explore our own brokenness as a prerequisite for healing and discover the deep wounds within us which must be lanced before they can heal. This exploration provides the ground of compassion for the brokenness of our fellow men and

14. Merton, *Wisdom of the Desert*, 18.

15. Merton, *Thomas Merton in Alaska*, 130–31.

even enables us to experience their sin as if it were our own. In his book *Gandhi on Non-Violence*, Merton offers this insight,

> In St. Thomas Aquinas, we find a totally different view of evil. Evil is not only reversible but is the proper motive of that mercy by which it is overcome and changed into good. Replying to the objection that moral evil is not the motive for mercy since the evil of sin deserves indignation and punishment rather than mercy and forgiveness, St. Thomas says that on the contrary sin itself is already a punishment "and in this respect we feel sorrow and compassion for sinners." In order to do this we have to be able to experience their sin as if it were our own. But those who "consider themselves happy and whose sense of power depends on the idea that they are beyond suffering any evil are not able to have mercy on others by experiencing the evil of others as their own."[16]

If we are in mystery, one body in Christ, we are also one body in brokenness. As we seek the integration of our body, mind, and soul, we become the source of integration and reconciliation for others. Animated by the Spirit, we increasingly become living sacraments of reconciliation for one another and become a force for unity and integration in the world. As we reorient ourselves to God, we reorient ourselves to the natural world and our relationships with our neighbors. We are assisted in this by Jesus who not only possessed the unique flesh of his body, born of Mary, but in mystery clothed himself with the flesh of all humanity. We are all one body, his family, reconciled through his intercession. We become the persons described in *Thomas Merton in Alaska* who realize that "the foundation of our life is that the Spirit is given and that we are led by the Spirit. Our life should flow from the presence of the Spirit in us, from the freedom of the Spirit in us."[17]

Living a life flowing from the presence of the Spirit within us, we assist step by step, and imperceptibly, in building up the kingdom of God. Our participation in this task is essential according

16. Merton, *Gandhi on Non-Violence*, 72.
17. Merton, *Thomas Merton in Alaska*, 77.

to Merton, who wrote in *The Recovery of Paradise*, "The world was created without man, but the new creation which is the true Kingdom of God is to be the work of God in and through man. It is to be the great, mysterious, theandric work of the Mystical Christ, the New Adam, in whom all men as 'one Person' or one 'Son of God' will transfigure the cosmos and offer it resplendent to the Father."[18]

In summary, we as the broken body of Christ seek healing through our individual and collective reconciliation. Through our growth in integration and wholeness, we grow in love and compassion. We heal as we are healed, and we become living sacraments of reconciliation, one to another. In the process, we share in the healing light generated by Christ on the cross, captured by a phrase in the song "Small Two of Pieces": "Broken mirror, a million shades of light."[19] However, there is even a greater degree of integration possible and a brighter and more mysterious light.

THE GREATEST LIGHT ARISES FROM NO MIRROR, NO LIGHT—JUST THIS!

Merton points the way. Within the confines of a monastery and his vocation as a monk, he journeyed in obedience to the guidance of the Spirit. It led him to the restoration of his true self and his unique identity in Christ. It led him to become a brother of God by knowing the "burnt men," which he learned through his identification with the suffering of the oppressed and the poor. It led him not only to reconciliation with God, but also to his neighbors of many cultures and religious traditions. It led him to global wisdom and to a final integration giving birth to a comprehensive self that accepts all mankind. In *Contemplation in a World of Action*, we read Merton's oft quoted description of final integration,

> The one who has attained final integration is no longer limited by the culture in which he has grown up. "He has embraced all of life." . . . He passes beyond all these

18. Merton, *Zen and the Birds of Appetite*, 132.

19. Mitsuda, "Small Two of Pieces."

limiting forms, while retaining all that is best and most universal in them, "finally giving birth to a fully comprehensive self." He accepts not only his own community, his own society, his own friends, his own culture but all mankind. He does not remain bound to one limited set of values in such a way that he opposes them aggressively or defensively to others. He is fully "Catholic" in the best sense of the word. He has a unified vision and experience of the one truth shining out in all its various manifestations, some clearer than others, some more definite and more certain than others. He does not set these partial views up in opposition to each other, but unifies them in a dialectic or an insight of complementarity. With this view of life he is able to bring perspective, liberty and spontaneity into the lives of others. The finally integrated person is a peacemaker, and that is why there is such a desperate need for our leaders to become such persons of insight.[20]

Integrated persons, such as Merton, appear open to the unity and traces of wisdom which speak to them through nature, other individuals, other cultures, and other religions. Merton communicates, through his journals, books, and correspondence, an openness to global wisdom, "which is the one truth shining forth in all of its manifestations,"[21] wherever it may be found. His search for that one truth appears to be a vital part of his vocation, expressed in his wish to reconcile to some extent these disparate traditions by deeply entering into them and reconciling them within himself. Merton elaborates on his desire in *Merton and Buddhism*,

> To emphasize, clarify the living content of spiritual traditions, especially Christian, but also the Oriental, by entering myself deeply into their disciplines and experience, not for myself only but for all my contemporaries who may be interested and inclined to listen. This is for the restoration of man's sanity and balance that he may

20. Merton, *Contemplation in a World of Action*, 207.
21. Merton, *Contemplation in a World of Action*, 207.

return to the ways of freedom and of peace, if not in my time, at least some day soon.[22]

Similarly, we find the scholar A. M. Allchin writing on this aspect of global wisdom in Merton's vocation:

> Here we find Merton beginning to realize something of the catholicity, the universality of the human person, discovering his own vocation to become, through the power of the Holy Spirit, that truly universal catholic person whom we see at the end of his life. His vocation is to cross frontiers, to cross frontiers in time, searching back into the past, and to cross barriers in space, barriers of language and culture and political situation and deep historical prejudice. We see here his sense that he is called to unite in himself the vision, the experience, the understanding of many times and many places, to hold them together in one and to share them with his own contemporaries.[23]

As a fruit of this openness to global wisdom, Merton explodes with creativity and spontaneity in his works, prototypical of the Zen man. It is the spontaneity and dance of the Spirit in creation, moving with minimal impediments in the fully integrated person. As Jesus proclaims, "The wind blows wherever it pleases. . . . That is how it is with all who are born of the Spirit."[24] And it can blow a responsive individual like Merton into some unexpected corners.

Merton's intellectual, artistic, and spiritual enquiries, as well as his receptivity to global wisdom, were truly vast. For example, through the gaze of his interior, Shaker architecture was seen as an expression of the sacred. He could say, "Among the Sioux Indians, together with a very rich and varied liturgical life, we find the curiously moving individual and contemplative mystery of crying for a vision,"[25] or "It is well known that in the Orient, in China, India, Japan, and Indonesia, the religious and contemplative life

22. Montaldo and Henry, *Merton and Buddhism*, 141.

23. Allchin, "Thomas Merton and the Christian East," 130.

24. John 3:8.

25. Merton, *Inner Experience*, 29.

has been fostered for centuries and has known a development of unparalleled richness."[26] Following this global wisdom, in his lecture in Bangkok immediately before his death, he declared,

> And I believe that by openness to Buddhism, to Hinduism, and to these great Asia traditions, we stand a wonderful chance of learning more about the potentiality of our own traditions, because they have gone, from the natural point of view, so much deeper into this than we have. The combination of the natural techniques, and the graces and the other things that have been manifested in Asia and the Christian liberty of the gospel should bring us all at last to that full and transcendent liberty which is beyond mere cultural differences and mere externals— and mere this or that.[27]

Although unaware of his destination as a young monastic, Merton chronicled his journey in faith as its light led him in new and creative paths to experience the global wisdom of other religions and Zen ideas. He sought to integrate and reconcile in himself the truths of these other traditions as a forbearer of unity among mankind at a deep spiritual level. His was an ever expanding retreat from a false self with its illusions to a recovery of his true self, which realized that we had to recover what we already are: at our deepest core there is no mirror or light, "just this" immersion of our being in Love, where we are already one. In a talk in Calcutta near the end of his life, Merton emphasizes this point: "My dear brothers, we are already one. But we imagine that we are not. And what we have to recover is our original unity. What we have to be is what we are."[28]

At the core of Merton's monastic journey was his ever deepening union with Christ and Christ's prayer, "May they all be one,"[29] in which Christ's petition to his Father assures its fulfillment in responsive hearts. As early as July 4, 1952, Merton, in

---

26. Merton, *Inner Experience*, 29.

27. Merton, *Asian Journal*, 343.

28. Merton, *Asian Journal*, 308.

29. John 17:7–21.

his poetic essay "Fire Watch," speaks of his union with the Father, when he writes,

> You Who sleep in my breast, are not met with words, but in the emergence of life within life and of wisdom within wisdom. You are found in communion: Thou in me and I in Thee and Thou in them and they in me: dispossession within dispossession, dispassion within dispassion, emptiness within emptiness, freedom within freedom. I am alone. Thou art alone. The Father and I are One.[30]

As this union matured, Thomas Merton and Fr. Louis (Merton's ordained name) vanished into the solitude of God. In getting lost in God, Merton became lost to himself. Writing in *The Monastic Journey*, Merton speaks of the relationship of a hermit to God:

> Beyond and in all this, he possesses his solitude, the riches of his emptiness, his interior poverty; but of course, it is not a possession. It is an established fact. It is there. It is assured. In fact, it is inescapable. It is everything—his whole life It contains God, surrounds him with God, plunges him in God. So great is his poverty that he does not even see God; so great are his riches that he is lost in God and lost to himself. He is never far enough away from God to see Him in perspective, or as an object. He is swallowed up in Him, and therefore, so to speak, never sees Him at all.[31]

This profound solitude hollowed him out, deepening his interior poverty and emptiness. He illustrates this point by describing the prayer life of the hermit as a profound unknowing of himself, of beating his head against the roots of his own existence. He writes in *The Monastic Journey*,

> All day and all night, the hermit beats his head against a wall of doubt. That is his contemplation . . . a kind of unknowing of himself, a kind of doubt that questions the very roots of his existence, a doubt which undermines his very reasons for existing and for doing what he does. It is

30. Merton, *Sign of Jonas*, 361–62.

31. Merton, *Monastic Journey*, 20.

this doubt that which reduces him finally to silence, and in the silence which ceases to ask questions, he receives the only certitude he knows; the presence of God in the midst of uncertainty and nothingness as the only reality.[32]

Beating his head against the very roots of his existence, Merton appears on the threshold of a complete emptiness which he may have realized on his final trip to Polonnaruwa, Sri Lanka, where the giant statues evoked an interior explosion, causing him to exclaim, "Everything is emptiness and everything is compassion."[33] In such an empty person, there would be no mirror to reflect light or brokenness to generate light, "just this" very ground of life, itself. (Incidentally, Merton characterized Nirvana in an essay published the year of his death as "Absolute Emptiness is Absolute Compassion."[34])

Such a person may also have attained perfect prayer. Saint Anthony describes perfect prayer when he states that "the prayer of the monk is not perfect until he no longer realizes himself or the fact that he is praying."[35] Similarly in *Zen and the Birds of Appetite*, Merton suggests, "In either case the highest illumination of love is an explosion of the power of Love's evidence in which all the psychological limits of an 'experiencing' subject are dissolved and what remains is the transcendent clarity of love itself, realized in the ego-less subject in a mystery beyond comprehension but not beyond consent."[36]

Merton provides us with a Zen-like description of the effect of this profound emptiness in his description of the parable of the wise virgins in Matthew.[37] He writes of departing from this emptiness,

32. Merton, *Monastic Journey*, 206–7.

33. Merton, *Asian Journal*, 235.

34. Merton, *Zen and the Birds of Appetite*, 86.

35. Merton, *Wisdom of the Desert*, 8–9.

36. Merton, *Zen and the Birds of Appetite*, 86–87.

37. Matt 25:1–4.

> But it is an activity of faith that belongs to our realm of
> knowledge, and conditions us for a superior and more
> vigilant innocence: the innocence of the wise virgins
> who wait with lighted lamps, with an emptiness that is
> enkindled by the glory of the Divine Word and enflamed
> with the presence of the Holy Spirit. That glory and that
> presence are not objects which "enter into" emptiness to
> "fill" it. They are nothing else but God's own "suchness."[38]

It is *just this* suchness which radiates a brilliant light in those like the wise virgins. In *Merton and Hesychasm*, we find Merton's description of the light emanating from those who seek to unite the wisdom of God in things with the light of wisdom within themselves in meditation on *theoria*—the ancient Greek word for contemplation. Merton writes,

> Man by *theoria* is able to unite the hidden wisdom
> of God in things with the hidden light of wisdom in
> himself. The meeting and marriage of these two brings
> about a resplendent clarity within man himself, and
> this clarity is the presence of Divine wisdom fully rec-
> ognized and active in him. Thus man becomes a mirror
> of the divine glory and is resplendent with divine truth
> not only in his mind but in his life. He is filled with the
> light of wisdom which shines forth in him, and thus
> God is glorified in him. At the same time he exercises a
> spiritualizing influence in the world by the work of his
> hands which is in accord with the creative wisdom of
> God in things and in him.[39]

A visitor to Saint Seraphim, a Russian hermit, describes how blinding that light may be. When he was asked by Saint Seraphim to look at him, he says, "I cannot look . . . because lighting is flashing from your eyes. Your face has become brighter than the sun, and my eyes ache with pain."[40]

From this visitor's description, it would appear that this light is brighter than that of those who have polished their interior

38. Merton, *Zen and the Birds of Appetite*, 133.

39. Dieker and Montaldo, *Merton and Hesychasm*, 157.

40. Serafim, *St. Seraphim of Sarov*, 99.

mirror in finding their true selves or those who are further along the path who radiate the light of a broken mirror through their compassionate union with Christ's suffering in humanity. For, no light emerges from them except God's own light, which is the light of the Holy Spirit. As Merton writes of Saint Seraphim and this light in *Mystics and Zen Masters*,

> An apprehension of the invisible as visible insofar as all creation is suddenly experienced as transfigured in a light for which there is no accounting in terms of any philosophy, a light which is given directly by God, proceeds from God, and in a sense is the divine Light. Yes, this experience is not a substantial vision of God, because in Oriental theology the light experienced by the mystic is a divine "energy," distinct from God's nature but which can be apprehended in contact with the Person of the Holy Spirit, by mystical love and grace.[41]

> In directly encountering "God's own suchness," this visitor encountered the divine energy as a blinding light emanating from the Holy Spirit.[42]

It is the light seen by the apostles on Mount Tabor,[43] and the light perceived by those whose fidelity to the Spirit has given them eyes to see. I believe that Thomas Merton was one of those persons who had eyes to see—*just this.*

41. Merton, *Mystics and Zen Masters*, 182.

42. Merton, *Zen and the Birds of Appetite*, 133.

43. Matt 17:2.

6

Attending to the Presence of God

Thomas Merton and le Point Vierge

WE ENCOUNTER THOMAS MERTON'S realization of *le point vierge*, the hidden point at the center of the true self where the spirit toucheds God, through the copious meditations which flow from his journals and books. He empties himself in self-revelation as he pours himself out onto the page with lines, which transform into hot brands to sear the mind that encounters them. Emanating from this virginal point, those lines share the spiritual quest of this monk, prophet, and social activist—this seeker of the no-face of the living God. As if on a flowing river, his lines carry us on a meditative barge through his youth, his monastic life, his journey to the East, his death. They cascade like a waterfall flowing from its source at *le point vierge* and, if we enter into their contemplative rhythm, they could ferry us to God.

Thomas Merton's poetic prose propels us on this journey as he trumpets,

> Here is an unspeakable secret. Paradise is all around us and we do not understand. It is wide open. The sword is taken away, but we do not know it: we are off "one to his farm and another to his merchandise." Lights on. Clocks

ticking. Thermostats working. Stoves cooking. Electric shavers filling radios with static. "Wisdom," cries the dawn deacon, but we do not attend.[1]

Heeding the cries of the dawn deacon, Merton silently attends to the presence of God to become a transparent messenger of wisdom, born in solitude, and encourages us to embrace paradise through our own pursuit of wisdom. In this chapter, I reflect on some of Thomas Merton's writings, which focus on his attending to the presence of God, in the hope that in doing so we may bear the fruit in us of knowing that all around is paradise. To know this, we must ask, *What prevents us from realizing that all around is paradise? If our false self is the barrier, what are the means to the recovery of our true self? What is the true self?*

Merton teaches that we have a choice of two identities: the external mask of our false self or a true self which can attend to the presence of God. Of this, he writes,

> We have the choice of two identities: the external mask which seems to be real and which lives by a shadowy autonomy for the brief moment of earthly existence, and the hidden, inner person who seems to us to be nothing, but who can give himself eternally to the truth in whom he subsists. It is this inner self that is taken up into the mystery of Christ, by His love, by the Holy Spirit, so that in secret we live in Christ.[2]

What prevents us from realizing that all around is paradise? Our choice of an exterior mask or our false self, originating in sin and fruitlessly questing to be a god, blinds us. Authored by original sin and sustained by our infidelities to reality, the false self centers relationships on itself and estranges us from God and consequently from others, as well as the natural world. At its core, this false self wishes to be a god; Merton writes,

> We seek what one might call a relative omnipotence: the power to have everything we want, to enjoy everything

1. Merton, *Conjectures of a Guilty Bystander*, 132.
2. Cunningham, *Thomas Merton*, 255.

> we desire, to demand that all our wishes be satisfied and
> our will should never be frustrated or opposed . . . It is a
> radical falsity which rots our moral life in its very roots
> because it makes everything we do more or less a lie.[3]

This radical falsity births a selfhood that God does not know
and, according to Merton, that is altogether too much privacy.[4]
This external mask creates a lens through which one falsely sees
creation only in relationship to oneself, and which separates us
from the reality of creation.[5]

Arising from our true self, an interior voice accuses us of this
infidelity to our innermost being and to God, generating a struggle
within. We drown that voice by engaging in distractions. In a world
of overwhelming sensory barrage, we should be reminded of Merton's view that these distractions suppress our discontent and delay
the confronting of our false self. We thereby delay facing our self-
hate arising from the lie we make of our lives. Merton writes,

> And behind the smokescreen of amusements and proj-
> ects, the inner dissatisfaction marshals all its forces for
> a more terrible assault when the distraction shall have
> been taken away. At last, the spirit that has fled from
> itself all its life, is stripped of its distractions at death
> and finds itself face to face with what can no longer be
> avoided; there is nothing now to prevent it from hating
> itself utterly, and totally, and forever.[6]

Merton existentially views this false self to be a cramp of non-
entity and nothingness that leads to despair. Merton infers that "in
the end, as we realize more and more that we are knotted upon
nothing, . . . the cramp is a meaningless, senseless, pointless affirmation of non-entity . . . a makeshift identity which is nothing."[7] Merton goes on, "What he really seeks and needs—love, an authentic
identity, a life that has meaning—cannot be had merely by willing

3. Merton, *Silent Life*, 13–15.

4. Merton, *New Seeds of Contemplation*, 33.

5. Merton, *Conjectures of a Guilty Bystander*, 294.

6. Merton, *Monastic Journey*, 101.

7. Merton, *Conjectures of a Guilty Bystander*, 224.

and by taking steps to procure them."[8] What cannot be achieved by willing can be received as a gift if we are open to it. Merton insists, "In order to be open, we have to renounce ourselves, in a sense we have to die to our image of ourselves, our autonomy, our fixation upon our self-willed identity. We have to be able to relax the psychic and spiritual cramp which knots us in the painful, vulnerable, helpless 'I' that is all we know as ourselves."[9] Although our false self barricades our realization, our true self touching God at *le point vierge* knows that indeed all around is paradise.

What are the means to the recovery of our true self? The Holy Spirit through the modalities of prayer, grace, silence, and solitude leads us to the recovery of our true self.

The journey to our true self entails a life of prayer. Merton believes prayer leads us to our center where we can experience the mercy of God.[10] It opens the door to self-knowledge, which allows the Holy Spirit to shine upon the alleyways of our dark interior.[11] Prayer leads us to union with God and communion with others.[12] Prayer allows the community to touch God and God to touch the community. For Merton, "The mind that prays in me is more than my own mind, and the thoughts that come up in me are more than my own thoughts because this deep consciousness when I pray is a place of encounter between myself and God and between the common love of everybody."[13]

The recovery of our true self requires grace. Merton observes, "Once we find ourselves in the state of 'knowledge of good and evil' we have to accept the fact and understand our position, see it in relation to the innocence for which we were created, which we have lost and which we can regain."[14] Grace restores our innocence through the promptings of the Holy Spirit, our source of grace, our

---

8. Merton, *Conjectures of a Guilty Bystander*, 224.

9. Merton, *Conjectures of a Guilty Bystander*, 224.

10. Merton, *Thomas Merton in Alaska*, 160.

11. Merton, *Thomas Merton in Alaska*, 160–61.

12. Merton, *Thomas Merton in Alaska*, 136.

13. Merton, *Thomas Merton in Alaska*, 135.

14. Merton, *Zen and the Birds of Appetite*, 128.

guide, and our destination. Realizing that the "only source of the spiritual life is the Holy Spirit,"[15] Merton believes grace prompts us to seek the truth of ourselves and our lives as we seek the Truth that is God.

Through grace, we recover our true self by the work of Christ in us who transforms us by shrouding himself with the wounds of our sins. Merton states, "The Christ we find in ourselves is not identified with what we vainly seek to admire and idolize in ourselves—on the contrary, He has identified himself with what we resent in ourselves, for He has taken upon Himself our wretchedness and our misery, our poverty and our sins."[16] By actualizing the recovery of our hidden identity in him, Christ transforms our self-hate to love, promoting peace within us and thereby with others.[17] Through the power of the Holy Spirit, grace liberates us from sin's creation, the false self.

Silence and solitude allow us to relax the psychic and spiritual cramp of our lives to immerse ourselves in the mystery of our identity in God, for "when we are quiet, not just for a few minutes, but for an hour or several hours, we may become uneasily aware of the presence within us of a disturbing stranger, the self that is both I and someone else."[18] Silence is healing since "silence makes us whole if we let it."[19] Silence guides us to the solitude of our true self and the ground of our being where we encounter God and peace.[20] In this solitude, the inner door of one's heart opens, allowing the Spirit to flow and Love to be spoken.[21]

In our journey to our true self, Merton cautions against particular ways or methods. Instead, he suggests we cultivate an attitude of openness:

---

15. Merton, *Contemplation in a World of Action*, 271.

16. Merton, *Monastic Journey*, 102.

17. Merton, *Monastic Journey*, 101.

18. Merton, *Essential Writings*, 74.

19. Merton, *Essential Writings*, 77.

20. Merton, *Essential Writings*, 77.

21. Merton, *Essential Writings*, 78.

> An "outlook": faith, openness, attention, reverence, ex-
> pectation, supplication, trust, joy. All these finally perme-
> ate our being with love in so far as our living faith tells us
> we are in the presence of God, that we live in Christ, that
> in the Spirit of God we "see" God our Father without see-
> ing. We know him in "unknowing." Faith is the bond that
> unites us to him in the Spirit who gives us light and love.[22]

What is the true self? Merton believes our true self is our real but hidden identity in Christ, in which our spirit and God's spirit become one. This point of union is *le point vierge*, which is the hiding place of God within us, inaccessible to our meddling but realized by those who see God through grace and purity of heart. By the recovery of our innocence before God, we see through spiritual eyes that paradise is all around, that every point is equidistant to God, that God's light shines through the natural world, and a blazing light like a diamond resides in everyone. Our true self fosters a life without care, a life of peace and union with others, and communications that become communion.

In Merton's view, the Spirit leads us to the core of our being and awakens us to our true identity in Christ: "Each one of us, in some sense, is able to be completely transformed into the likeness of Christ, to become, as He is, divinely human, and thus to share His spiritual authority and charismatic power in the world."[23]

When we come to know our true self, we, in some degree, have returned to paradise as a new person with a measure of the innocence present before the fall. Merton states, he "who has realized in himself purity of heart . . . has been restored in some measure to the innocence lost by Adam."[24] Merton's experience at the corner of Fourth and Walnut in Louisville, Kentucky, where he realized that he was not alien to the strangers around him, reflects this innocence. Through the lens of his recovered true self, he realizes *le point vierge* as a point of poverty and nothingness that is

22. Finley, *Merton's Palace of Nowhere*, 93.
23. Merton, *Inner Experience*, 38.
24. Merton, *Zen and the Birds of Appetite*, 131.

the Glory of God within us. Consequently, he sees other persons radiating a heavenly light.[25] Merton writes,

> At the center of our being is a point of nothingness which is untouched by sin and by illusion, a point of pure truth, a point or spark which belongs entirely to God . . . This little point of nothingness and of absolute poverty is the pure glory of God in us . . . It is like a pure diamond, blazing with the invisible light of heaven. It is in everybody, and if we could see it we would see these billions of points of light coming together in the face and blaze of a sun that would make all the darkness and cruelty of life vanish completely . . . I have no program for this seeing. It is only given. But the gate of heaven is everywhere.[26]

In writing of this experience, Merton uses the phrase *le point vierge*, which has its origin in the teachings of a ninth century Sunni mystic, Al-Hallaj. Al-Hallaj taught that the core of the human heart was accessible only by God, but that our spirit may touch God at the virginal center of this core, *le point vierge*. At the time of his experience at Fourth and Walnut, Merton was reading the writings of Al-Hallaj as popularized by Massignon, with whom Merton corresponded.

The recovery of the true self awakens us to the mystery of the presence of God. For Merton, an initial awareness of this presence led him to the Catholic Church: "My conversion to Catholicism began with the realization of the presence of God in this present life, in the world and myself, and that my task as a Christian is to live in full and vital awareness of this ground of my being and of the world's being."[27] Through the church with her liturgy and sacraments, he found the grace to break through his false self to his true identity in Christ.

As we attend to the presence of God, the spirit mothers us into a spiritual being that grows in union with God. That is, "the spiritual awakening of mind and heart . . . is an awareness that we

25. Merton, *Conjectures of a Guilty Bystander*, 158.

26. Merton, *Conjectures of a Guilty Bystander*, 158.

27. Merton, *Conjectures of a Guilty Bystander*, 158.

are not merely our everyday self, but we are also one with One who is beyond all human and individual self-limitation."[28] This spiritual rebirth is continuous, beginning on earth and growing with the intensity of our union with God. For Merton, "The true Christian rebirth is a renewed transformation, a 'passover' in which man is progressively liberated from selfishness."[29] We become one flame burning with an ever increasing brightness.

To find the presence of God within ourselves, we do not need to journey into strange lands or seek some exotic vantage point. For "we do not need to leave the point where we are and seek it [God's presence] somewhere else, but to forget all points as equally irrelevant because to seek the unlimited in a definite place is to limit it and hence not to find it."[30] The only relevant point is the center of ourselves in which we "return to the heart, finding one's deepest center, awakening the profound depths of our being in the presence of God who is the source of our being and our life."[31] It is our encounter with this presence that accelerates our maturity as persons of God. Before this presence, "all the burdens of our autonomous self disperse."[32]

The interior journey to our true self and God is reserved for all. Also, the availability of this deep presence of God and mystery in Christ at the center of our being is not limited to the professed Christian. Merton declares that "I honestly think that there is a presence of Christ to the unbeliever . . . The Lord who speaks of freedom in the ground of our being still continues to speak to every man."[33]

By attending to the presence of God, Thomas Merton bore "immense fruit in the souls of men [he] will never see on earth."[34] That fruit manifests itself in us as we engage with him by entering

28. Merton, *Essential Writings*, 65.

29. Merton, *Essential Writings*, 66.

30. Finley, *Merton's Palace of Nowhere*, 127.

31. Finley, *Merton's Palace of Nowhere*, 99.

32. Finley, *Merton's Palace of Nowhere*, 139.

33. Merton, *Conjectures of a Guilty Bystander*, 326.

34. Merton, *Seven Storey Mountain*, 462.

into the contemplative rhythm of his words. Much more than just receiving the instruction of his writings, we are caught up in his contemplative experience and brought to our own ever deepening realization of the presence of God. His prayerful writings are animated by the union of his spirit with that of God. Through them, the Holy Spirit can direct our spiritual formation, deepen our attention to the presence of God, and awaken us to the transparent mystery of God shining through all. Merton tells us,

> The thing that we have to face is that life is as simple as this. We are living in a world that is absolutely transparent, and God is shining through it all the time . . . You cannot be without God. It's impossible, it's just simply impossible. The only thing is that we don't see it. This again is what we are here for.[35]

The Holy Spirit also can deepen our communications with one another, becoming a communion through which we recover our unity. "And the deepest level of communication is not communication, but Communion . . . we are already one."[36]

We, like Merton, can aspire to become transparent bearers of God's presence and radiate the flame of God's love to enkindle the hearts of others. Through our encounters with them, we may awaken to realize Merton's insight that "we are already one . . . and what we have to recover is our original unity."[37] We may seek to build in our own communities the monastic ideal of persons in contact with God, radiating his presence and peace into the world where we create "a new creation, an earthly paradise in which God once again dwells with men and is almost visibly their God, their peace and their consolation."[38]

Attending to the presence of God in our lives will bring us to peaceful union and unity with our brothers and sisters and allow

35. Merton, *Essential Writings*, 70.

36. Merton, *Asian Journal*, 308.

37. Merton, *Asian Journal*, 308.

38. Merton, *Monastic Journey*, 66–67.

us to see the "one truth shining forth in all of its manifestations."[39] If we heed the cries of the dawn deacon, we, like Thomas Merton, will attend to global wisdom and recover our true self.

39. Merton, *Contemplation in a World of Action*, 207.

7

A Certain Victory

Thomas Merton and the
Journey of Personhood

THIS ESSAY EXPLORES THE writings of Thomas Merton in regard to our journey in personhood. For Merton, the essence of personhood derives from our being made in the image and likeness of God, which is to emulate the image and likeness of the personhood of Jesus Christ. The more perfectly one adheres to this image, the more perfectly one is a person. Merton considers Adam, who was made in the image and likeness of God, to be an archetype of personhood for humankind. After his fall and estrangement from God, his personhood diminished as his likeness to God diminished.

Consequently, personhood is dynamic, and one may be growing into fuller personhood or receding. For us to grow in personhood we must seek to recover our likeness to Christ, which is the recovery of our true self. We recover our true self through Christ's merciful redemptive act. Consequent to the passion and resurrection of Christ, the Holy Spirit saturates humankind with grace, restoring the image and likeness of God within us by increasing our likeness to Christ. Through our receptivity to the grace arising from the mercy of Christ we grow in communion with the Spirit of God, which is the foundation of our communion with others.

In *The New Man*, Merton writes extensively about Adam as a person made in the image and likeness of God who has a relationship to God as his son. "Adam was created not merely as a living and moving animal who obeyed the command and will of God. He was created as a 'son' of God because his life shared something of the reality of God's own breath or Spirit."[1] Merton agrees with Saint Augustine that "the "image of God is found in the soul's structure—awareness, thought, love"[2] and uses the illustration of a photograph to explain the concepts of image and likeness. Merton writes,

> A blurred photograph of a person is a picture or an image of the person, but it is overexposed or double-exposed or otherwise defective. A clear photograph is not only a picture of the person but is a "likeness" of the person, giving an exact idea of him. And so, Saint Augustine says, "In this image (which is the soul) the resemblance of God will be perfect when the vision of God is perfect."[3]

As a consequence of being made in God's image and likeness, Adam is in communion with God and creation. Through this contemplative gaze, creation, in a sense, worships God. Merton suggests, "It was in the sounding solitude of Adam's understanding that things without reason became able to adore their creator."[4] But by sacrificing Adam's solitude, God creates human society in creating Eve, so that Adam is not only in communion with God and creation, but he is also in communion with another human person. Merton suggests, "Adam, perfectly whole and isolated in himself, as a person, needs nevertheless to find himself perfected, without division or diminution, by the gift of himself to another. He needs to give himself in order to gain himself."[5] The garden of Eden thus symbolizes a person's integrative wholeness manifested

1. Merton, *New Man*, 46–47.
2. Merton, *New Man*, 54–55.
3. Merton, *New Man*, 54–55.
4. Merton, *New Man*, 64.
5. Merton, *New Man*, 101.

by Adam and Eve's personal relationship with God and their innocent relationship with creation and one another.

Solely through his communion with God could Adam remain in communion with Eve and creation. Hence, Merton views the consequences of the fall of Adam as catastrophic for humankind because humankind is contained in a mysterious fashion within Adam. With the fall, the image of God within humankind is darkened and the likeness to God obscured. Adam, and thereby humankind, becomes alienated from God. Relationships with God, neighbor, and creation are fractured. As a consequence of Adam's prideful choice to know evil, the resulting spiritual deformity begets enmity between neighbors and promotes humankind's exploitation of creation. Pride branded humankind with the desire to know unreality. As Merton writes, "For pride is a stubborn insistence on being what we are not and never were intended to be. Pride is a deep, insatiable need for unreality, an exorbitant demand that others believe the lie we have made ourselves believe about ourselves. It infects at once man's person and the whole society he lives in. It has infected all men in the original pride of Adam."[6]

Pride is the source of the egocentric or false self. Merton distinguishes the person from this mask created by the ego, when he writes, "It is a great mistake to confuse the person (the spiritual and hidden self, united with God) and the ego, the exterior, empirical self, the psychological individuality who forms a kind of mask for the inner and hidden self. This outer self is nothing but an evanescent shadow. Its biography and its existence both end together at death."[7]

To grow in personhood, we must seek the recovery of our true selves, which is to grow in the image and likeness of Christ. For Merton, this requires grace, virtue, and asceticism. He writes,

> To reach one's "real self" one must, in fact, be delivered by grace, virtue and asceticism, from that illusory and false "self" whom we have created by our habits of selfishness and by our constant flights from reality. In order to find

6. Merton, *New Man*, 113.

7. Merton, *New Seeds of Contemplation*, 279.

God, whom we can only find in and through the depths of our own soul, we must therefore first find ourselves. To use common figures of speech, we must "return to ourselves," we must "come to ourselves."[8]

The recovery of this real self requires the Holy Spirit, our source of grace, our guide, and our destination. Through grace, we recover our true self by the work of Christ-in-us who transforms us by shrouding himself with the wounds of our sins. Merton states, "The Christ we find in ourselves is not identified with what we vainly seek to admire and idolize in ourselves—on the contrary, He has identified himself with what we resent in ourselves, for He has taken upon Himself our wretchedness and our misery, our poverty and our sins."[9] By actualizing the recovery of our hidden identity in him, Christ transforms our self-hate to love, which promotes peace within us and thereby with others. Merton observes, "The peace which Christ brings is the outcome of this war faced and fought on earth: man's war with himself, in which (by God's grace) he overcomes himself, conquers himself, pacifies himself, and can at last live with himself because he no longer hates himself."[10] Through the power of the Holy Spirit, grace liberates us from sin's creation, the false self which includes not only the ego but the tyrannical superego. Merton writes,

> Grace is given us for the precise purpose of enabling us to discover and actualize our deepest and truest self. Unless we discover this deep self, which is hidden with Christ in God, we will never really know ourselves as persons. Nor will we know God. The "self" to which grace is opposed is not merely the passionate, disordered, confused self—the rambling and disheveled "ego"—but much more the tyrannical "super-ego," the rigid and deformed conscience which is our secret god and which with an

---

8. Merton, *New Man*, 72.

9. Merton, *Monastic Journey*, 102.

10. Merton, *Monastic Journey*, 101.

infinitely jealous resourcefulness defends its throne
against the coming of Christ.[11]

The recovery of our true self promotes growth in our personhood as we grow in love, recovering our identity in Christ. For
Merton, it is the light of the resurrection, which enables this fuller
expression of our personhood. In the *Road to Joy*, he writes, "The
power of the Resurrection is the power of love. . . . Let us be one in
this love, and seek to make all men one in it, even here on earth."[12]
The power of the resurrection is the power for us to develop our
identity in Christ as persons conjoined to the divine. Through his
death, resurrection, and the outpouring of the Holy Spirit, the law
that Christ brings is no less than the living energy of Love that
propels our integration as unique persons who journey to recover
the divine image and likeness of God within us, and in doing so
love one another. Merton views our transformed true inner self as
an immortal person when he tells us, "The true inner self, the true
indestructible and immortal person, the true 'I' who answers to a
new and secret name known only to himself and to God."[13]

Through the light of the resurrection, we have the opportunity to experience transforming union with Christ and become a
temple for the indwelling of the Father, Son, and Holy Spirit. The
recovery of our image and likeness restores us to our sonship or
daughterhood with the Father. This is not an imaginary adoption
but an entry into a very real relationship with the life of the Father,
Son, and Holy Spirit. The light of the resurrection, which is the
love of Christ, births us into this deeper personhood, propelling
us into communion with God and neighbor. In this sense, Christ's
death and resurrection, through which the Holy Spirit is poured
upon us, enables us to be gradually birthed into a more perfect
personhood. The Spirit transforms us progressively, conjoining
our spirit to his. We are thus more or less a person depending
upon the extent to which we are filled with the Spirit of Christ and,

11. Merton, *New Man*, 49–50.

12. Merton, *Road to Joy*, loc. 2449.

13. Merton, *New Seeds of Contemplation*, 279.

through him—communion with the Divine Persons. The fruit of this union is growth in love, which Merton perceives to be the task of personhood and the meaning of true Christianity.

True Christianity is growth in the life of the Spirit, a deepening of the new life, a continuous rebirth, in which the exterior and superficial life of the ego-self is discarded like an old snakeskin and the mysterious, invisible self of the Spirit becomes more present and more active. The true Christian rebirth is a renewed transformation, a "passover" in which man is progressively liberated from selfishness and not only grows in love but in some sense "becomes love. . . . To become completely transparent and allow Love to shine by itself is the maturity of the 'New Man.'"[14]

Thus, growth in personhood requires the recovery of the true self as manifested by our progress in the restoration of our image and likeness to God through becoming more intimately united with Christ. This growth is super-animated by the light of the resurrection, which is the outpouring of the love of Christ so that one is propelled toward the love of God and neighbor. For Merton, this allows us to be fully human, as he writes,

> Love is, in fact, an intensification of life, a completeness, a fullness, a wholeness of life . . . Life curves upward to a peak of intensity, a high point of value and meaning, at which all its latent creative possibilities go into action and the person transcends himself or herself in encounter, response, and communion with another. It is for this that we came into the world—this communion and self-transcendence. We do not become fully human until we give ourselves to each other in love . . . We do not find the meaning of life by ourselves alone—we find it with another.[15]

In his book *God Is Not a Christian*, Bishop Tutu echoes this sentiment through the African notion of *ubuntu*, when he writes, "A person is a person through other persons. *Ubuntu* teaches us that our worth is intrinsic to who we are. We matter because we

14. Merton, *Love and Living*, 199.

15. Merton, *Love and Living*, 26.

are made in the image of God. *Ubuntu* reminds us that we belong in one family—God's family, the human family."[16] In Merton's and Bishop Tutu's view, communion in relationships is essential to our personhood. A person is one in communion with another, and it is communion that leads to union. Christ references this communion and unity when he says, "Father, may they be one in us, as you are in me and I am in you."[17]

Persons seeking communion form communities with varying degrees of holiness as determined by the intensity of communal love. The holy family models a holy community in which Mary is so intimately united to the Spirit of God that the Christ child is formed in her womb while Joseph unselfishly provides sustenance and offers fatherly protection. The child who grows in wisdom and grace as true God and true man bridges mankind to the Godhead by his indwelling presence first within Mary and then within humanity. Through Christ the holy family is interwoven with the life of the Trinity, and this holy community begets others. As a result, families and monastic communities have the potential for great degrees of holiness. However, the degree of holiness in such communities depends upon the extent that their members penetrate to their true self and thereby enter the ground of love through which individuals are in communion.

Merton clearly expresses this transformation into the fullness of personhood when he writes in *Love and Living*,

> But it is by our decision as persons, that is, by our belief, our acceptance of life in the person of Christ, our response as persons to his personal and saving love, that our manhood is seized and transformed by the life-giving Spirit. Thus, Christ is born in our nature that we may be reborn in the fullest sense as persons. The full Christian sense of the person is found in the recovery of our likeness of God, in Christ, by his Spirit.[18]

16. Tutu, *God Is Not a Christian*, 21–23.

17. John 17:21.

18. Merton, *Love and Living*, 226.

The perfection of personhood is found in Christ, whose being both fully human and fully divine is not only the perfect image and likeness of God but also the source of our own growth in personhood. Through Christ's redemptive act—birth, death, and resurrection—the Holy Spirit mercifully saturates humankind with grace, ensuring a certain victory in our own journey of personhood.

This new law of God written in our hearts is a law of mercy enacted by the very presence of the Holy Spirit, enabling us to be healed, to love, and to grow as persons. This is evident when Merton writes,

> "What are the (new) laws of God written in the hearts of men," Augustine asks, "if not the very presence of the Holy Spirit?" Hence, the Law of Mercy is not an extrinsically given imperative but an inner power, not an inexorable demand imposed on a weak and confused nature but a personal inclination to love imparted by the presence of the Spirit of Sonship who makes us free, liberating us from the tyranny of natural weakness and of existential demands for self-assertion. The whole climate of the New Testament is one of liberation by mercy: liberation, through God's grace and free gift, from sin, death, and even from the Old Law. The miraculous acts of Christ in the synoptics tend generally to make this clear. The power of forgiveness is clearly associated with the power of healing and restoring to life.[19]

This point is further illuminated when, as a young monk, Merton encountered this mercy: "What was cruel has become merciful. What is now merciful was never cruel. I have always overshadowed Jonas with my mercy, and cruelty I know not at all. Have you had sight of Me, Jonas, my child? Mercy within mercy within mercy. I have forgiven the universe without end, because I have never known sin."[20]

It is this mercy that guarantees a certain victory in our journey to personhood because mercy is healing. Merton believes, "It

19. Merton, *Love and Living*, 209.

20. Merton, *Love and Living*, 216.

heals bodies, spirit, society, and history."[21] Brought through the horrors of the cross, mercy restores us into the image and likeness of God and elevates us to a divine life in communion with God and neighbor. As Merton writes,

> It is the only force that can truly heal and save. It is the force that has been brought into the world in the great eschatological event of the Cross, in order that man might be totally renewed, and that the guilt-ridden and despairing *Dasein* of the lost human person might find itself reconciled in freedom and mercy with the needs and destinies of others and of the world itself. Mercy heals the root of life by curing our existence of the self-devouring despair which projects its own evil upon the other as a demand and an accusation.[22]

In his *Misericordiae Vultus: Bull of Indiction of the Extraordinary Jubilee of Mercy*, Pope Francis proclaims, "Mercy: the word reveals the very mystery of the Most Holy Trinity. Mercy: the ultimate and supreme act by which God comes to meet us . . . Mercy: the bridge that connects God and man, opening our hearts to the hope of being loved forever despite our sinfulness."[23] This law of mercy *as* love written within our hearts is the integrating principle of our personhood, and its effect is to progressively integrate us into deeper union with the Persons of God—Father, Son, and Holy Spirit. A human person, then, is a human being propelled by this indwelling merciful love to seek wholeness by the integration of body, mind, and soul to be in communion with God and neighbor.

In this Jubilee Year, a unique door of overflowing mercy has been opened to assist us in our journey into a more mature personhood. It is a door of God's limitless love and mercy made manifest in the coming of Christ. It is a door that passes through the cross and pierces the heart of the Father, releasing a mercy so blinding that God as Father only sees created beings through the lens of the image and likeness of his Son. It is a door of mercy that

---

21. Merton, *Love and Living*, 216.

22. Merton, *Love and Living*, 216.

23. Francis, *Misericordiae Vultus*.

Pope Francis proclaims to be "the fundamental law that dwells in the heart of every person who looks sincerely into the eyes of his brothers and sisters on the path of life."[24] In this Year of Mercy, may we seize the grace to open that door and pass through it.

24. Francis, *Misericordiae Vultus*.

8

Thomas Merton and Saint John of the Cross

Lives on Fire[1]

THE STREETS WERE EMPTY that cold day as we shivered in our spring clothes. In January, no one is in Ubeda, not even American tourists! We were there almost by happenstance at a convenient place to spend the night on the long drive back to Madrid from Grenada. My family chose a trip to southern Spain, foolishly thinking it would be warmer than other European destinations. (My unsolicited advice would be that if you plan to take a trip to southern Spain in January, take your ski clothes!) Our trip included a rail excursion to Toledo and a self-driving tour through Andalusia, including visits to Seville and Granada.

As we set out to explore the town, my middle son, an insatiable explorer, stumbled across a museum with the name of Juan de la Croix and asked whether I had heard of him. The museum was the monastery where Saint John died. After touring the restored cell in which he lived, we viewed his relics and the table on which they treated his gangrenous leg. Unaware, I had traced

1. Originally published in *Merton Annual*, 205–13.

his movements in southern Spain (where he tirelessly journeyed to establish and serve in monasteries) and awakened to the reality of our own "pilgrimage" one day before departing Spain. It is this reawakened interest in the writings of Saint John of the Cross coupled with the long-term assistance provided by that spiritual guide, Thomas Merton, which prompts this essay.

In this essay, I wish to share some observations about Thomas Merton and Saint John of the Cross as persons on fire with the love of God. I will do this using Saint John of the Cross's concept of contemplation as an encounter with the fiery presence of God. I intend also to reflect on the end effects of such a contemplation expressed by Merton as "the unity of a person" or "final integration" and Saint John as "The Living Flame of Love."

Both Thomas Merton and Saint John of the Cross encountered the God Moses described in Deuteronomy as a consuming fire.[2] The analogy of God as fire permeates most of Saint John's writings, especially in writing about the *Dark Night of the Soul* and the *Living Flame of Love.*

Saint John views the contemplative process as the transformation of the soul by this consuming fire. The source of this fire—the Spirit—afflicts, transforms, and causes the soul to blaze in loving union with the Father and the Son. Merton also experienced this fire, as illustrated through his description of himself as a burnt man, his reference to "the living experience of divine love and Holy Spirit in the flame of which Saint John of the Cross speaks"[3] and believing that this spark resides in our heart. Like Saint John, Merton viewed contemplation as the action of the Spirit within the heart of every person. God's embrace of contemplatives such as Thomas Merton and Saint John of the Cross cause them to be burnt, purged, and erupt into flames. Although both roared into flames, their writings reflect an individual, personal, and unique expression of each's union with God.

In his writings, Merton quotes extensively from the texts of Saint John and acknowledges his debt to him as a spiritual forbearer

2. Deut 4:24.

3. Merton, *Contemplative Prayer*, 88.

and guide. Early in his monastic life, Merton comments on his relationship to Saint John, "I say that St. John of the Cross seems to me to be the most accessible of the saints, that is only another way of saying that he is my favorite saint."[4] Merton saw Saint John as accessible because he revealed his inner depths and the intimacy of his relationship with God for all to see. As Merton writes,

> Nevertheless it is true, if you consider that few saints, if any, have ever opened up to other men such remote depths in their own soul. St. John of the Cross admits you, in the Living Flame, to his soul's "deepest center," to the "deep caverns" in which the lamps of fire, the attributes of God, flash mysteriously in metaphysical shadows; who else has done as much?[5]

I think many of us would answer: Thomas Merton, who undressed himself, his thinking, his reflections, and contemplative journey, in full public view.

These men, who were possessed by God and dispossessed in so many other ways, had many similarities during their earthly pilgrimage but also some striking differences. Both had splintered families at an early age. Juan de Yepes y Alvarez, who would become Saint John of the Cross, was born in Fontiveros, Spain, in 1542, the son of an affluent father who was disowned for marrying beneath his station. He died shortly after John's birth, forcing John's mother to support the family by silk weaving. Like John, Merton lost a parent at a young age. He was six when his mother died of stomach cancer.

Saint John had a reputation of piety from youth and at age seventeen attended a Jesuit College while working at the Plague Hospital de la Concepcion. After being ordained in 1567 in the Carmelite order, he later joined Saint Teresa as her confessor and spiritual director at the Convent of the Incarnation. Saint Theresa introduced John to members of her convent as a saint. By contrast, devoted readers are quite familiar with the more Augustinian youthful life of Thomas Merton, particularly while at Cambridge,

4. Luce, *Saints for Now*, 274.

5. Luce, *Saints for Now*, 274.

which may have been influenced by the bohemian lifestyle of his artistic father. At age seven, Merton was traveling in the company of his father and his father's love interest, including her husband, to Bermuda.

Both Saint John's and Merton's spiritual lives thrived in the desert. In 1576, the Calced Friars arrested John and confined him to a small cell in their monastery in Toledo because of his reform efforts. During this time of physical confinement and abuse, he composed the "Spiritual Canticle," reflecting a spirit on fire. In the confinement of a Trappist monastery, Merton became a two-fisted monk. He took to being a monk the way he formerly took to the bars: He went at it. He left nothing behind, taking with him all of his gifts—writing, scholarship, and a mind that would follow the truth wherever it took him. Within the monastery, Merton became an explorer of himself, society, other cultures, and the no-face of God.

Both experienced rejection. Although Saint John held many offices in the Discalced Province and tirelessly journeyed on foot in their service, he was rejected by his own order, which threatened to send him to Mexico near the end of his life. Shortly afterward, when Saint John's leg became infected, he chose to go to the monastery at Ubeda where his humility moved a hostile prior to become a champion of Saint John's cause for beatification. Likewise, Merton was rejected by many as he spoke out for social justice and the peace movement and immersed himself in Eastern thought.

While their lives were similar in some respects and very different in others, it is in the writings of their experience of the Spirit that their kinship is most striking. Both were great spiritual writers, guides, and passionate men who sought God with great desire. Thomas Merton experienced the purgation reflected in Saint John of the Cross's metaphor of the soul being like a log of wood heated by an external flame before slowly igniting and roaring into flames. Saint John described this process in the *Dark Night of the Soul*:

> For the greater clearness of what has been said, and of what has still to be said, it is well to observe at this point that this purgative and loving knowledge or Divine

light whereof we here speak acts upon the soul which it is purging and preparing for perfect union with it in the same way as fire acts upon a log of wood in order to transform it into itself; for material fire, acting upon wood, first of all begins to dry it, by driving out its moisture and causing it to shed the water which it contains within itself. Then it begins to make it black, dark and unsightly, and even to give forth a bad odour, and, as it dries it little by little, it brings out and drives away all the dark and unsightly accidents which are contrary to the nature of fire. And, finally, it begins to kindle it externally and give it heat, and at last transforms it into itself and makes it as beautiful as fire.[6]

In *The Ascent to Truth*, Merton uses a similar fiery analogy:

It is into this abyss of blazing light, so infinitely bright as to be pure darkness to our intelligence that the mystic enters not only with his eyes, his imagination, and his mind but with his whole soul and substance, in order to be transformed like a bar of iron in the white heat of a furnace. The iron turns into fire. The mystic is "transformed" in God.[7]

Merton also alludes to this purgation at the end of *The Seven Storey Mountain* when he quotes the Spirit as speaking to him:

Everything that touches you shall burn you, and you will draw your hand away in pain, until you have withdrawn yourself from all things. Then you will be all alone. Everything that can be desired will sear you, and brand you with a cautery, and you will fly from it in pain to be alone. Every created joy will come to you as pain, and you will die to all joy and be left alone. You will be praised, and it will be like burning at the stake.[8]

6. John of the Cross, *Complete Works*, 402–3.

7. Merton, *Ascent to Truth*, 261.

8. Merton, *Seven Storey Mountain*, 462.

Merton concludes the revelation on why he was brought to Gethsemani: "That you may become the brother of God and learn to know the Christ of the burnt men."[9]

Becoming the brother of God led him into some strange places and activities as he became the brother of every person. After his epiphany on the streets of Louisville in 1958, he reached out to his brothers everywhere including celebrities, social activists, and Buddhist and Zen monks. He also experienced the Christ of the burnt men, in himself, his neighbors, those who immolated themselves during the Vietnam peace protest, and in his death by electrocution. But most of all, he knew the Christ of the burnt men purged by the fire of contemplation. Purged by that fire, Merton's soul roared into flames. In one of his last written testimonies, *Contemplative Prayer*, he wrote,

> The living experience of divine love and Holy Spirit in the flame of which St. John of the Cross is speaking is a true awareness that one has died and risen in Christ. It is an experience of mystical renewal, an inner transformation brought about entirely by the power of God's merciful love, implying the "death" of the self-centered and self-sufficient ego and the appearance of a new and liberated self who lives and acts "in the Spirit."[10]

Saint John described what that liberated self who lives and acts in the Spirit experiences.

This flame of love is the Spirit of its bridegroom, which is the Holy Spirit. The soul feels him within itself not only as a fire that has consumed and transformed it but as a fire that burns and flares within it, as I mentioned. And that flame, every time it flares up, bathes the soul in glory and refreshes it with the quality of divine life.[11]

Experiencing this flame, Merton wrote, "Love sails me around the house . . . I have only time for eternity which is to say for love, love, love . . . it is love and it gives me soft punches all the

9. Merton, *Seven Storey Mountain*, 462.

10. Merton, *Contemplative Prayer*, 88.

11. John of the Cross, *Collected Works*, 580.

time in the center of my heart."[12] Merton attained a liberated self who lives and acts in the Spirit or "a living flame of love" in Saint John's verbiage.

Although both were burnt by the same Spirit, their fruition differed toward their spiritual journey's end. While Merton chose to emphasize the Spirit's effect on leading a person to integration and wholeness, Saint John focused on the intensity of the Spirit's flame. From Merton's perspective, the contemplative as a living flame of love recovers the true self, obtains final integration, and has a realization of oneness with God and all that is. Merton states such a person embraces all of humanity, transcending the accidents of culture, and recognizes the one truth shining out in all of its manifestations:

> The one who has attained final integration is no longer limited by the culture in which he has grown up. "He has embraced all of life . . ." He passes beyond all these limiting forms, while retaining all that is best and most universal in them, "finally giving birth to a fully comprehensive self." He accepts not only his own community, his own society, his own friends, his own culture, but all mankind. He does not remain bound to one limited set of values in such a way that he opposes them aggressively or defensively to others. He is fully "Catholic" in the best sense of the word. He has a unified vision and experience of the one truth shining out in all its various manifestations, some clearer than others, some more definite and more certain than others. He does not set these partial views up in opposition to each other, but unifies them in a dialectic or an insight of complementarity. With this view of life he is able to bring perspective, liberty and spontaneity into the lives of others. The finally integrated person is a peacemaker, and that is why there is such a desperate need for our leaders to become such persons of insight.[13]

However, Merton is no stranger to the divine love operating within the soul. He writes that the fruit of contemplation results in a new

12. Merton, *Thomas Merton Reader*, 190.

13. Merton, *Contemplation in a World of Action*, 207.

man in union with the Spirit of Christ and therefore one with the Father and Spirit. He states that our oneness with Christ consists of being united to his Spirit, writing, "We cannot get too deep into the mystery of our oneness in Christ. It is so deep as to be unthinkable and yet a little thought about it doesn't hurt. But it doesn't help too much either. The thing is, that we are not united in a thought of Christ or a desire of Christ, but in His Spirit."[14] He perceives contemplation, like Saint John of the Cross, as the very act of this living flame, the Spirit, bringing us into union with the Father by purifying our hearts. The fruit of this purgation is love.

That is to say, he loves with purity and freedom that spring spontaneously from the fact that he has fully recovered the divine likeness and is now his fully true self because he is lost in God and hence knows of no ego in himself. All he knows is love.[15]

Near the end of Merton's life, the yearning of that Spirit flared from the depths of his heart as he spontaneously uttered the closing prayer at a conference in Calcutta.

> We are creatures of love. Let us join hands, as we did before, and I will try to say something that comes out of the depths of our hearts. I ask you to concentrate on the love that is in you, that is in us all. I have no idea what I am going to say. I am going to be silent a minute, and then I will say something . . . O God, we are one with you. You have made us one with you. You dwell in us. Help us to preserve this openness and to fight for it with all of our hearts. Help us to realize that there can be no understanding where there is mutual rejection. Oh, God, in accepting one another wholeheartedly, fully, completely, we accept You, and we thank You, and we adore You, and we love You with our whole being because our being is in Your being, our spirit is rooted in your Spirit. Fill us then with love, and let us be bound together with love as we go our diverse ways, united in this one spirit which makes You present in the world, and which makes You witness

14. Merton, *Hidden Ground of Love*, 360.

15. Merton, *Thomas Merton Reader*, 487.

to the ultimate reality that is love. Love has overcome.
Love is victorious. Amen.[16]

Although both men's writings testify to similar qualities in
their experience of union with God's Spirit, it does not appear to
me that Merton communicates (or chooses to communicate) the
intensity of the Spirit's wounding love that Saint John calls a cautery. Saint John notes that a soul in union with God can experience
an even hotter flame, when he writes,

> This cautery, as we mentioned, is the Holy Spirit. For
> as Moses declares in Deuteronomy, Our Lord God is a
> consuming fire [Deut 4:24], that is, a fire of love which,
> being of infinite power, can inestimably consume and
> transform into itself the soul it touches. Yet He burns
> each soul according to its preparation. He will burn one
> more, another less, and this He does insofar as He de-
> sires, and how and when He desires. When He wills to
> touch somewhat vehemently, the soul's burning reaches
> such a high degree of love that it seems to surpass that
> of all the fires of the world, for He is an infinite fire of
> love. As a result, in this union, the soul calls the Holy
> Spirit a cautery. Since in a cautery the fire is more intense
> and fierce and produces a more singular effect than it
> does in other combustibles, the soul calls the act of this
> union a cautery in comparison with other acts, for it is
> the outcome of a fire so much more aflame than all oth-
> ers. Because the soul in this case is entirely transformed
> by the divine flame, it not only feels a cautery, but has
> become a cautery of blazing fire.[17]

It is true that Thomas Merton is no Saint John of the Cross.
But then again, Saint John of the Cross is no Merton. Each man
was shaped by his embrace of God to become uniquely himself.
Merton's personality flared toward openness, tolerance, inclusive-
ness, and wholeness. His intellect questioned and integrated. He
stretched boundaries and saw "the one truth shining forth in all of
its manifestations." He saw beyond irreconcilable differences and

16. Merton, *Asian Journal*, 318–19.

17. John of the Cross, *Collected Works*, 596.

viewed the disparate as complementary. Buddhism, Zen, Sufism, existential literature, art, photography, and all objects of his contemplative gaze as well as his lived experiences complemented his journey as a Christian contemplative. To my thinking, one of his major accomplishments was to achieve final integration in himself as a prophetic sign pointing the way toward a potential deeper union of humankind, which may be attainable despite all our disparate cultures and belief systems.

Saint John's temperament and mission differed. A reformer, confessor, and spiritual guide during his lifetime, Saint John's mission was to poetically communicate the soul's embrace by God. He was uniquely gifted to view, experience, and communicate the Spirit's effect on his own soul to the furthest extent possible and still remain on earth. A spiritual guide to Saint Teresa of Avila and Merton, he beckons to those who leave all paths as they are consumed by the fire of the living God.

Separated by time, culture, and mission, both contemplatives, in the Spirit, share with us their journey to God. For a fractured world bent on destruction, Merton radiates hope with his message of "the unity of a person" and "final integration," whereas Saint John explains the timeless process of transforming union in which God and man become one "Living Flame of Love."

In conclusion, I propose that Thomas Merton like Saint John of the Cross became a living flame of love. Purged by the Spirit of God, both penetrated into the center of their being to become a roaring conflagration as only occurs in those brought to union with the living God. Burnt by this fire, both wrote of its effect. Merton's concept of the person, "a unity which is love," and his concept of the person's "final integration" arose from this encounter as did Saint John of the Cross's perception of the perfected person as a "living flame of love."

Finally, for both men, contemplation is the means to this encounter. Merton states, "Contemplation is a supernatural love and knowledge of God, simple and obscure, infused by Him into the summit of the soul, giving it a direct and experimental contact with him."[18] Saint John indicates that contemplation perfects the soul so that it may experience the indwelling of the Holy Trinity. An effect of this indwelling for Merton is the final integration of the person: "He has a unified vision and experience of the one truth shining out in all its various manifestations."[19] Similarly, Saint John relates that a perfected soul "knows creatures through God and not God through creatures."[20] Saint John would agree with Merton that "the one love that is the source of all, the form of all, and the end of all is one in him and in all."[21] Both encountered that love and became living flames spewing embers catching others on fire.

18. Merton, *Inner Experience*, 73.

19. Merton, *Contemplation in a World of Action*, 207.

20. John of the Cross, *Collected Works*, 645.

21. Merton, *Love and Living*, 17.

9

Stand on Your Own Feet!

Thomas Merton and the Monk without Vows or Walls[1]

"From now on, Brother, everybody stands on his own feet,"[2] proclaims Thomas Merton on the day of his death. He was quoting an abbot who gave this advice to the Tibetan monk Chogyam Trungpa Rimpoche, confronted with fleeing or staying in the face of an advancing Chinese communist army. Merton interprets this saying to be "an extremely important monastic statement" and asserts that "the time for relying on structures has disappeared."[3] This essay explores the concept of a monk standing on his own feet without walls or vows. Traditionally, we view the monk as someone enclosed by physical boundaries, adhering to a particular spiritual tradition, and bound by vows. However, stripped to its essentials, what constitutes the vocation of a monk? Can its essence be hidden within any vocation? With Merton as guide, this essay focuses on the basic elements of being a monk both for those in the monastery and for those in the world. It considers the visible

---

1. Originally published in *Merton Annual*, 154–68.

2. Merton, *Asian Journal*, 338.

3. Merton, *Asian Journal*, 338.

monks in the world such as the lay monk Brother Wayne Teasdale, those of the New Monasticism, and the New Friars, as well as more hidden, invisible monks. Concentrating on Merton's thoughts in regard to purity of heart and reconciliation, the chapter will review the transformational process which molds all monks and guides them to "final integration."[4]

AN ATYPICAL TRADITIONAL MONK

Thomas Merton is a model of a traditional although atypical monk who stands on his own feet. Secluded behind the walls of a monastery, he continues his vocation as a writer. His yearning for the freedom of solitude leads him into a hermitage. He advocates for peace by publicly decrying the Vietnam War and railing against the atomic bomb. He joins the civil rights movement. He studies Eastern religions. Through his writings and actions, he reflects someone who stands on his own feet, arrives at his own conclusions, and speaks the truth with the light that he is given. On the surface, he appears to be an anomaly—an outspoken monk afloat in the cultural waters of the Cistercian tradition—who bridges monastic isolation through diverse activities, including a dialogue with people of good will from various faiths, traditions, and cultures, and rendezvous with the famous, such as Joan Baez. Although he shatters the iconic image of a monk, Merton personifies an authentic selfhood congruent with his interior convictions, a man of integrity. From him, we learn that monks who live from the center of their authenticity reveal their true self, which is the image and likeness of God, uniquely expressed through their personhood as it exists at a particular place and time in history. For Merton, this meant integrating within himself other cultures, traditions, and religions as he sought to expand his interior boundaries to become more inclusive, as expressed in his comments on "final integration:"

> The man who has attained final integration is no longer
> limited by the culture in which he has grown up. "He has

4. Merton, *Contemplation in a World of Action*, 205–17.

embraced all of life . . ." He passes beyond all these limiting forms, while retaining all that is best and most universal in them, "finally giving birth to a fully comprehensive self." He accepts not only his own community, his own society, his own friends, his own culture, but all mankind.[5]

Merton realizes that the human race in all its diversity is the body of Christ and that all of creation pulsates at its core with the energy of the divine. "We must, first of all, see all material things in the light of the mystery of the incarnation. We must revere all creation because the word was made flesh."[6] For Merton, the monk with this realization has begun his journey to attain final integration, which is not a discovery of the mind through words or images but an exploration of the heart.

He was a Trappist monk living in a monastery, within the enclosed walls of Our Lady of Gethsemani Abbey, at least most of the time. He was fed by the silence and solitude of a monastery, which was "a tabernacle in the desert, upon which the shekinah, the luminous cloud of the divine Presence, almost visibly descends."[7] He felt both nourished and restrained by his environment. His writings suggest that at times he was dancing with angels, as when he proclaims, "Love sails me around the house. I walk two steps on the ground and four steps in the air. It is love."[8] On deep issues of conscience, he appears bridled by convention and the arbitrary whims of his superiors and censors, as illustrated by his lament to James Forest in the Cold War letters: "The orders are, no more writing about peace. This is transparently arbitrary and uncomprehending."[9] However, of greater importance, he was bound by ascetic vows:

> The whole ascetic life of the monk, in all its aspects both positive and negative, is summed up in his consecration of himself, his whole life, all that he has and all that he is,

5. Merton, *Contemplation in a World of Action*, 212.

6. Merton, *Monastic Journey*, 18.

7. Merton, *Silent Life*, 34.

8. Merton, *Sign of Jonas*, 120.

9. Merton, *Hidden Ground of Love*, 266.

> to God, by his five monastic vows. The life of the monk
> is the life of the vows . . . Conversion of manners means
> striving to change one's whole life and all one's attitudes
> from those of the world to those of the cloister . . . Obedi-
> ence means the renunciation of our own will, in order
> to carry out in our whole life the will of another who
> represents God. Stability means renouncing our freedom
> to travel about from place to place, and binds us to one
> monastery until death. Poverty and Chastity are not
> explicitly mentioned in the Rule of St Benedict because
> they were considered by him to be included in conver-
> sion of manners, but they form an essential part of the
> monk's obligations.[10]

Particularly during his hermetic solitude, these vows challenged
him to the very depths of his existence:

> The hermit, all day and all night, beats his head against a
> wall of doubt. That is his contemplation . . . a kind of un-
> knowing of his own self, a kind of doubt that questions
> the very roots of his existence, a doubt which under-
> mines his very reasons for existing and for doing what
> he does. It is this doubt which reduces him finally to
> silence, and in the silence which ceases to ask questions,
> he receives the only certitude he knows: the presence of
> God in the midst of uncertainty and nothingness, as the
> only reality.[11]

In this desert, Merton disappears (perhaps foreshadowing
his last publicly spoken words before he was electrocuted)[12] and is
"swallowed up in" God.[13] In union with the Holy Spirit, his liberated spirit radiates a creative openness to others, reaching fruition
in his speech in Calcutta when he says, "We are already one . . .
And what we have to recover is our original unity."[14] Transcending the limits of monastic formalism, a transformed Merton can

10. Merton, *Monastic Journey*, 30–31.

11. Merton, *Monastic Journey*, 159.

12. Merton, *Asian Journal*, 343.

13. Merton, *Monastic Journey*, 159.

14. Merton, *Asian Journal*, 308.

ask, "Can there be a monastic life without vows? Is a monastic life with vows necessarily better and more authentic than one without vows?"[15] He continues with this observation, "In the earliest days of desert monasticism, there were no vows, no written rules, and institutional structure was kept at a minimum. The monastic commitment was taken with extreme and passionate seriousness, but this commitment was not protected by juridical sanctions or by institutional control."[16] Merton is "convinced that a monastic life without vows is quite possible and perhaps very desirable. It might have many advantages."[17] He wonders, "Why could not married people participate temporarily, in some way, in monastic life?"[18] Finally, he questions the very structure of monasticism: "A greater flexibility in the monastic structure would permit the development of ecumenical monastic communities. There is no reason why non-Catholics and even unbelievers should not be admitted to a serious participation—at least temporary—in monastic community life."[19]

In *A Monastic Vision for the Twenty-First Century*, several prominent authors reflect on the future of monasticism with a focus on traditional monastic communities. As a group, they concentrate less on the form of future monastic communities and more on the guiding principles that will shape monastic life. For Michael Casey, these guiding principles are to be seekers of God, to radically renounce the world, and to live simply and within a spiritual tradition.[20] Bonnie Thurston believes the monk's pursuit of purity of heart is an indispensable ingredient of all future monasticism.[21] Joan Chittister thinks future monks must distinguish the concept of cloister, "as if place were the determining factor in the making of a contemplative," from that of contemplation, "as if

15. Merton, *Contemplation in a World of Action*, 191.

16. Merton, *Contemplation in a World of Action*, 191–92.

17. Merton, *Contemplation in a World of Action*, 191–92.

18. Merton, *Contemplation in a World of Action*, 192.

19. Merton, *Contemplation in a World of Action*, 195.

20. Hart, *Monastic Vision*, 24–25.

21. Hart, *Monastic Vision*, 75.

Jesus was not a 'contemplative,' as if all of us are not called to be contemplative."[22]

By contrast, Gail Fitzpatrick would retain monastic enclosure for its value "of guarding one's heart."[23] John Eudes Bamberger's "vision of Cistercian life for the twenty-first century is the monastery as a school of charity where all the essential, practical skills for attaining to union with God are acquired."[24] He views the task of the monk as "the recovery of the likeness to the Word of God" achieved "by developing the whole of our person, including the spiritual senses."[25] Similarly, Francis Kline views the lifetime work of the monk both now and in the future to be that of suffering and dying with Christ so that through the power of the Holy Spirit there is "the formation of the Risen Christ in the heart of a monk."[26] Although Merton would agree with all of these viewpoints, he appears to transcend the boundaries of traditional monasticism when he states that monastic life without vows may be desirable, married persons could participate, and non-believers would be welcomed. In doing so, Merton points us to non-traditional monks.

VISIBLE NON-TRADITIONAL MONKS

Wayne Teasdale: A Hermit in the City

As if in response to Merton's musings, self-declared monks in the world appear after Merton's death. One of these, Brother Wayne Teasdale, referred to himself as a hermit in the city. Influenced by both Merton and Abbot Thomas Keating in the 1960s, Brother Wayne was no ordinary hermit secluded from others; he taught at a number of institutions, including Catholic Theological Union in Chicago. After living in an ashram in India for two years, he became a Christian sannyasi under the influence of Bede Griffiths,

22. Hart, *Monastic Vision*, 95.

23. Hart, *Monastic Vision*, 150.

24. Merton, *Love and Living*, 126–27.

25. Merton, *Love and Living*, 144.

26. Merton, *Love and Living*, 180.

who explained to him that "the real challenge for you, Wayne, is to be a monk in the world, a sannyasi who lives in the midst of society, at the very heart of things."[27] In 1989, the Archbishop of Chicago formally professed him to be a lay monk.

A contemplative, Brother Wayne was active in a variety of social issues such as the cause of the Dalai Lama, homelessness, and protecting the environment. He also espoused interfaith understanding through "interspirituality" which he viewed as the commonality of mystical experiences in diverse religions. He defines a monk as "a person who has dedicated his or her life to seeking God."[28] Teasdale asserts, "The daily tasks of earning a living, paying bills, saving money, getting along with others, being entertained, enjoying healthy recreation, and learning how to interact with difficult people are all part of an active life. So they must also be part of life for a monk in the world, at the crossroads of contemporary culture and experience."[29] For monks in the world, he suggests, "the question becomes how to integrate their glimpse of monastic peace into their everyday lives in the world, how to cultivate contemplation within an active life."[30] He thinks, "To achieve this integration requires the realization that the real monastery exists within them as a dimension of their own consciousness."[31] According to Brother Wayne, the structure of "monasticism in all its forms—Eastern, Western, primitive, inventive, contemplative, active, and mixed—exists to nurture the development, fruition, and gifts of the inner mystic or inner monk."[32] He espouses Keating's pronouncement that "the essence of monastic life is not its structures but its interior practice, and the heart of interior practice is contemplative prayer."[33]

27. Teasdale, *Monk*, xxii.

28. Teasdale, *Monk*, xxvi.

29. Teasdale, *Monk*, xxiv.

30. Teasdale, *Monk*, xxvi.

31. Teasdale, *Monk*, xxvi.

32. Teasdale, *Monk*, xxvii.

33. Teasdale, *Monk*, xxvii.

Similar to the desert fathers who went out to the desert and were tested by demons, Brother Wayne thinks that "in our age, the desert is the city—that is civilization."[34] He desires that there be more monks in the world because, he believes, "a contemplative in the heart of the world has the opportunity to be aware of, to relate to, to touch and heal this suffering, to be a sign of love and hope to those who are so vulnerable in this difficult and indifferent world."[35] He advises those who wish to be monks in the world to focus their life of prayer on contemplative meditation, spiritual reading, the practice of nature, including walking and sky meditation, and allowing for silence and solitude.[36] He counsels that an effect of contemplation is to root out the hidden motivations in our unconscious, the seeds of selfishness and negativity, and to further our integration.[37] A monk transformed by contemplation can envision a society of compassion, mercy, and love and be the leaven to radically transform the world by transforming others and eliminating cultural and economic selfishness.[38]

Teasdale views Merton as a forerunner of interspirituality through his study and appreciation of Eastern spiritual classics. Brother Wayne believed, "Thomas Merton was perhaps the greatest popularizer of interspirituality. Not only did he acquaint his readers with the rich and vast tradition of Christian contemplation . . . but he opened the door for Christians to explore other traditions, notably Taoism, Hinduism, and Buddhism."[39] He also believes that Merton's notion that "we are already one . . . and what we have to recover is our original unity"[40] goes beyond our cultural, psychological, and religious differences, points to the future of monasticism, and is key to transforming the world. To enable this transformation, Brother Wayne envisions a universal order

34. Teasdale, *Monk*, 13.

35. Teasdale, *Monk*, 15.

36. Teasdale, *Monk*, 23–24.

37. Teasdale, *Monk*, 41.

38. Teasdale, *Monk*, 135.

39. Teasdale, *Mystic Heart*, 39.

40. Merton, *Asian Journal*, 308.

of mystics or contemplatives which would "include people from all traditions and no tradition at all. They would include young and old, men and women, certain and skeptical, confused and enlightened."[41]

New Monasticism

Teasdale's vision is illustrated in the New Monasticism movement. Although some of these communities date to the early 1970s, with a heritage going back to 1930, the term "New Monasticism" was popularized by Jonathan Wilson-Hartgrove in the 1990s. It is based on Dietrich Bonhoeffer's belief that "the restoration of the church will surely come only from a new type of monasticism which has nothing in common with the old but a complete lack of compromise in a life lived in accordance with the Sermon on the Mount in the discipleship of Christ."[42] In his brief book *Life Together*, Bonhoeffer discusses "directions and precepts that Scriptures provide us for our life together under the word."[43] He perceives Christianity as "community through Jesus Christ and in Jesus Christ."[44] Members of the community spend the day in fellowship with others in prayer and work and alone in meditation. This fellowship is important as Bonhoeffer cautions, "Let him who cannot be alone beware of community; let him who is not in community beware of being alone."[45] As speech is essential for life in community, silence is essential for solitude. In this fellowship, Bonhoeffer proposes an atypical ministry which he refers to as "the ministry of holding one's tongue,"[46] "the ministry of meekness,"[47]

41. Teasdale, *Monk*, 218.
42. Bonhoeffer, *Testament to Freedom*, 424.
43. Bonhoeffer, *Life Together*, 17.
44. Bonhoeffer, *Life Together*, 21.
45. Bonhoeffer, *Life Together*, 77.
46. Bonhoeffer, *Life Together*, 91.
47. Bonhoeffer, *Life Together*, 94.

"the ministry of listening,"[48] "the ministry of helpfulness,"[49] "the ministry of bearing,"[50] "the ministry of proclaiming,"[51] and "the ministry of authority."[52] For the community to have spiritual depth, each member must acknowledge his or her sinfulness and partake in confession to be reconciled one to another and each to God. On this point, Bonhoeffer writes, "Reconciled in their hearts with God and the brethren, the congregation receives the gift of the body and blood of Jesus Christ, and, receiving that, it receives forgiveness, new life, and salvation . . . The life of Christians together under the Word has reached its perfection in the sacrament."[53]

Following Bonhoeffer's call for this kind of communal fellowship, Wilson-Hartgrove proposes a new monasticism which would aim at healing fragmentation and eliminating the distinction of sacred and secular vocations. This would be accomplished by a small group of disciples who, through intense theological reflection and commitment, would lead contemplative and communal lives with a focus on hospitality and concern for the poor. Following this idea, in 2004, a number of existing communities formulated a rule of life, known as the "Twelve Marks." These marks include living at the margins of society, sharing economic resources, hospitality, just reconciliation, submission to the church, a formative process like a novitiate, nurturing common life, support for both celibate singles as well as married couples and children, communal geographical proximity of members, care of the local environment and support of local economies, peacemaking and conflict resolution, and commitment to a contemplative life.[54] Wilson-Hartgrove believes the work of a new monastic community "is to tend to a culture of grace and truth in the world."[55] Doing this requires a reliance on

48. Bonhoeffer, *Life Together*, 97.

49. Bonhoeffer, *Life Together*, 99.

50. Bonhoeffer, *Life Together*, 100.

51. Bonhoeffer, *Life Together*, 103.

52. Bonhoeffer, *Life Together*, 108.

53. Bonhoeffer, *Life Together*, 122.

54. Wilson-Hartgrove, *New Monasticism*, 39.

55. Wilson-Hartgrove, *New Monasticism*, 135–36.

the church, where "the church is called to be a people who love one another and make a life together, tending to a culture of grace in a world broken by sin."[56]

Similar to the Twelve Marks community, the Iona community and the Northumbria community, among many others, are examples of the new monasticism. The Iona community, as described by Ronald Ferguson in *Chasing the Wild Goose: The Story of the Iona Community*, had Celtic monastic roots. In 1938, the founder, Reverend George MacLeod, led a group of craftsmen to rebuild the ruined medieval Iona Abbey on a small rocky island in the Scottish Hebrides, founding a community in the process. For the first twenty years of its existence, the community's activity centered on this restoration project. Later it became a community "bound together by a rule of private prayer, economic sharing, and work for justice and peace."[57] This ecumenical community is concentrated in Scotland, England, and Wales, with full members numbering in the hundreds, but there are also associates and friends of the community across the world.

The Northumbria community's beginnings are traced to the relationships of John and Linda Skinner and Andy Raine in Northumberland, England, in the late 1970s and early 1980s. These relationships were followed by the creation of the Nether Springs Trust with the help of Roy Searle and Trevor Miller. With a geographically dispersed community, "They attempt to find a practical modern expression of a new monasticism rooted in the vows of 'availability and vulnerability' and hold an uncompromising allegiance to the imperatives of the Sermon on the Mount."[58] Members progress in stages from being postulants to novices and, finally, to full companions. They follow a rule of "availability," being available to God in the cell of their hearts as well as to others; "vulnerability," manifested as being teachable in prayer; and the "heretical imperative," by challenging assumed truth, living among others as "church without walls."

56. Wilson-Hartgrove, *New Monasticism*, 145.

57. Ferguson, *Chasing the Wild Goose*, 35.

58. Foster, *Sanctuary of the Soul*, 94.

The New Friars

Another expression of the impetus toward a new monasticism may be the "New Friars." As author Scott Bessenecker writes,

> We are at the front edge of another missional, monastic-like order made up of men and women, many of whom are in their twenties and thirties, burning with a passion to serve the destitute in slum communities of the developing world—not from a position of power but from alongside them, living in the same makeshift housing, breathing the same sewage-tainted air, subject to the same government bulldozers that threaten to raze their communities. They are new friars, flying just below our radar because they have not come under any single denominational or suprachurch banner.[59]

Like their historic counterparts, Bessenecker views this movement as having the same roots and reflecting the same qualities, which he describes as incarnational, devotional, communal, missional, and marginal. He writes, "Slum communities are kinds of chapels in which one can meet face to face with Christ in the dispossessed."[60] The new friars' spirituality revolves around Christ's pledge, "I tell you solemnly, in so far as you did this to one of the least of these brothers of mine, you did it to me."[61] Their vocation is lived out over months or years alongside the destitute, those who are garbage scavengers, sex workers, homeless, abused, and those who are dying.

For Brother Wayne Teasdale, the New Monastics and the New Friars appear to be heroic individuals who stand on their own feet, open to grace. They have responded to the invitation of Christ's Spirit to "follow me" as they serve Christ in their work with the poor and the marginalized. Although their numbers may be small, their hearts are large and their efforts, like mustard seeds, will have their fruition in the kingdom of God. These individuals are very

---

59. Bessenecker, *New Friars*, 16.

60. Bessenecker, *New Friars*, 87.

61. Matt 25:40.

visible monks in the world. But there are more invisible ones who, without vows or walls, live outwardly a very ordinary life.

INVISIBLE NON-TRADITIONAL MONKS

Merton's attestation on the day of his death—"from now on, Brother, everybody stands on his own feet . . . The time for relying on structures has disappeared"[62]—may herald the work of the Spirit generating invisible non-traditional monks without walls or vows or monastic structure. Invisible monks, called to contemplation and solitude, live and work in all strata of society. Their external circumstances appear to be like those of their neighbors. They may work, marry, have children, and socialize, while nourishing a hidden vocation to live a life of prayer and to dwell in God's presence. The path of their work in the world and that of their interior life may appear in conflict early in their spiritual journey, with time set aside for solitude and contemplation stolen from time set aside for family or work. Ideally, at some point the inner and outer paths join so that in both being and doing their whole life becomes a living prayer.

The hidden vocation of the invisible monk is the same as that of the professed; it is to dwell in God's presence through a life of prayer. All monks quest to see the face of the living God, and this steadfast pursuit, either inside or outside the walls of a monastery, either with or without vows, characterizes this individual as a monk. The quest of the invisible monk is that of all monks who desire to be transformed into a new creation in which the old person becomes a new one dwelling in the presence of God.

The monastic monk, assisted by vows, monastic practices, the office, the liturgy, and the support of his brothers, seeks God alone. However, even with monastic support, such a monk faces doubt, interior struggles, and obstacles to his pursuit. Similarly, a monk in the world faces these as well as worldly activities, which often seek to separate him from God. For the invisible monk without walls or

62. Merton, *Asian Journal*, 338.

vows or a rule guaranteeing time set aside for prayer, much of his life may be consumed by an occupation or worldly concerns, such as office politics or bills to pay. However, such a person discovers that the Spirit who calls one to contemplation also arranges time for silence and solitude. This individual with his whole life surrounded by the obstacles of a secular environment may find the core of his existence wound around the pursuit of the presence of God.

What sets both the visible and invisible monk apart from others is their focused response to the invitation of the Holy Spirit to pursue the beatitude, "Happy the pure in heart: they shall see God."[63] The means to this end is contemplation, a flight of the will, and a mind and heart oriented toward God. This lifetime journey begins with an acceptance to an invitation from the Holy Spirit to allow the divine fire of contemplation to burn in them. Like fire burning a log, this spiritual fire, as described by Saint John of the Cross, is oppressive to the soul as it burns away the grime and habits of sin.[64] This solitary work digs at the roots of sin and gives rise to self-knowledge of the interior division, strife, and self-hatred that results from sin. This fire uncovers the boundaries separating one from one's true self, from others, and from God. As the Spirit, through divine fire, breaks down these boundaries, monks open themselves more fully to the presence of God, particularly as it is expressed in the presence of others. This presence of God may be discerned not only in those like them but in those who differ, not only in Christians but in Buddhists and Muslims as well as agnostics and atheists—in all of creation and the family of man. The goal of a mature discernment would be to realize, as Merton did, that "we are already one," and, thus, we have to recover "what we are."[65]

Of course, the journey to this awareness may be turbulent, as monks falter and soar. They appear caught up in the liturgical cycle of the birth, death, and resurrection of Christ as he comes to be born, to die, and to rise in them as they live out their lives interpenetrated by sin and grace. Yet this spiritual work wrought

63. Matt 5:8.

64. John of the Cross, *Collected Works*, 350.

65. Merton, *Asian Journal*, 308.

in them by God's grace and his Spirit remains hidden from them. They see it dimly, but do not know its fruits. In fact, their way of living in the world may not make sense even to themselves. They question their sitting, their meditation, their contemplation, their leisurely gazing, and their dim awareness of the realization of the presence of God. They wonder about the futility of their existence as measured by the productivity of their more active brethren. Days, months, years, decades pass, and it seems like they have not even made a beginning in the spiritual life. However, they are at peace living this marginal life which appears to them to be not only marginal to the world but seemingly even marginal to God. They live in a no man's land at the interface between Eden, from where they witness the light of God emanating, and a redeemed world darkened by sin. Somehow through the merits flowing from Christ's sacrifice, they hope to participate in his mediation.

Christian monks participate in that mediation by their interior exploration in which they encounter not only their own heart, but the heart of mankind in which both grace and sin abound. Although they may be aware of the presence of God and the light of grace, they are also in contact with the darkness of sin and its destructive power in themselves, the world, and others. In some small measure, it is their mission to bring this darkness to the light of Christ. As a consequence of being a conscious meeting point of the light and darkness, monks seek reconciliation for themselves. In doing so, they become instruments of reconciliation for others. Theirs is a never-ending task. As they seek to discover the center of their true self, where they find God, the solitary journey into the center of their own heart becomes a journey into the center of mankind's darkened heart. In their journey, every arrival becomes another departure.

STAND ON YOUR OWN FEET

With each arrival and departure, monks increasingly learn to stand on their own feet. They do this by withdrawing from a false self, concentrating through solitude on the exploration of an inner realm in which they seek God.[66] In the process they deepen their capacity for obedience, faith, freedom, and love—all critical elements for monks to stand on their own feet before God.

Merton emphasizes that our false self originates in our disobedience to the call to be a true son or daughter of God. Our disobedience makes us afraid, so we hide like Adam. We hide from God, we hide from our true self, and we hide from others. We fear that we will be discovered, unmasked, unclothed, and be naked before the truth of God, which is God's truth in us. On this point, Merton tells us,

> The man and his wife heard the sound of Yahweh God walking in the garden in the cool of the day, and they hid from Yahweh God among the trees of the garden. But Yahweh God called to the man. "Where are you?" he asked. "I heard the sound of you in the garden," he replied. "I was afraid because I was naked, so I hid." "Who told you that you are naked?" he asked. "Have you been eating of the tree I forbade you to eat?"[67]

This false self is the lie of our self-creation which results from our profound refusal to be the image and likeness of God. This wound of the false self has roots extending back to the garden of Eden.[68] As noted by Father John Eudes Bamberger,[69] the restoration of this image and likeness is the primary defining task of the monk, whether living in the monastery or within the world, as the Bible tells us in Genesis, "God created man in the image of himself: in the image of God he created him, male and female he created them."[70]

Through obedience, the monk's task is to return to Eden, to return to the presence of God. The path to this restoration passes through a dark night of dread, which arises from the realization that one's external identity is inauthentic and illusionary. Merton observes, "The purpose of the dark night, as St. John of the Cross

---

66. Merton, *Disputed Questions*, 177–207.

67. Gen 3:8–13.

68. Merton, *New Man*, 50–68.

69. Hart, *Monastic Vision*, 144.

70. Gen 1:27.

shows, is not simply to punish and afflict the heart of man, but to liberate, to purify and to enlighten in perfect love. The way that leads through dread goes not to despair but to perfect joy, not to hell but to heaven."[71] At its secret roots, dread opens into faith. If one opts to live at the center of this dread, the dread itself becomes a school of faith. In this barren desert, faith blossoms within the obscure and opaque boundary between the ground of ourselves and the ground of our being, the interface between us and God.

Monks stand on their own feet through their growth in faith in God and dependence on him and through their growth in faith in their community and dependence on them. Through the gift of faith, monks encounter God whose love is their freedom. Merton suggests that monks through their journey in faith realize that God is the supporting ground of their existence.[72] They may discover this support is expressed through others in community. Often, it appears, God stands such persons on their own feet by allowing them to lean on the backs of others, those of family, friends, workplace, community, and church. However, paradoxically, the cement holding them in these relationships may dissolve as monks surrender their group identity for their unique individual identity. Later, these relationships may be recovered at a more profound level as they become more centered on God. They may even realize that "the soul knows creatures through God and not God through creatures"[73] as Saint John of the Cross informs us.

As monks receive the gift of dependence on others, they share with them the gift of presence, not only their own but that of the risen Christ. By their fidelity to the quest of seeking the face of the living God, their union with God, however limited, allows them to become a transparent bearer of God to others. Merton notes,

> The presence of God in His world as its Creator depends
> on no one but Him. His presence in the world as Man
> depends, in some measure, upon men. Not that we can
> do anything to change the mystery of the Incarnation in

71. Merton, *Contemplative Prayer*, 138.

72. Finley, *Merton's Palace of Nowhere*, 93.

73. John of the Cross, *Collected Works*, 645.

itself: but we are able to decide whether we ourselves, and that portion of the world which is ours, shall become aware of His presence, consecrated by it, and transfigured in its light. We have the choice of two identities: the external mask which seems to be real and which lives by a shadowy autonomy for the brief moment of earthly existence, and the hidden, inner person who seems to us to be nothing, but who can give himself eternally to the truth in whom he subsists. It is this inner self that is taken up into the mystery of Christ, by His love, by the Holy Spirit, so that in secret we live "in Christ."[74]

Through interior exploration, monks recover their true self by the intervention of the Holy Spirit. For those in monasteries as well as those in the world, the monk's journey entails a life of prayer, grace, silence, and solitude. Prayer exposes their interior through self-knowledge, allows the mercy of God to heal their interior wounds, and leads them to union with God and communion with others.[75] Grace liberates them from the false self through the actions of the Holy Spirit, who prompts them to seek the truth of themselves as they seek the Truth that is God. Grace restores the lost innocence of Eden through the promptings of the Holy Spirit—their source of grace, their guide, and their destination. Silence guides them to the solitude of their true self and the ground of their being through which they encounter God and peace.[76] Through their interior exploration, they are hollowed out and experience their emptiness. Merton perceives the depths of this emptiness to be pure freedom and love. He writes of it, "The character of emptiness, at least for a Christian contemplative, is pure love, pure freedom. Love that is free of everything, not determined by anything, or held down by any special relationship . . . This purity, freedom and indeterminateness of love is the very essence of Christianity."[77]

74. Merton, *New Seeds of Contemplation*, 295.

75. Merton, *Thomas Merton in Alaska*, 160–61.

76. Merton, *Love and Living*, 20–21.

77. Merton, *Contemplative Prayer*, 118–19.

To experience the reality that God became man that man may participate in the divine (so often expressed in the liturgy of Eastern rites) is the deepest aspiration of monks. Their whole solitary journey revolves around this notion. It forms the core of the "work of God" which has been traditionally expressed through the office, choir, and liturgy and assisted by monastic stability and their vows—all designed to facilitate an encounter with God, through which monks are transformed. The monk without walls or vows may incorporate some of these practices as well as other paths seeking the same result. All of these paths exist to provide the individual time, silence, and focus to seek God, to be transformed by God through grace, and through union with God to participate in his divinity, which is to participate in his love. Merton suggests,

> But in fact the Resurrection and Ascension of Christ, the New Adam, completely restored human nature to its spiritual condition and made possible the divinization of every man coming into the world. This meant that in each one of us the inner self was now able to be awakened and transformed by the action of the Holy Spirit, and this awakening would not only enable us to discover our true identity "in Christ," but would also make the living and Risen Savior present in us . . . Each one of us, in some sense, is able to be completely transformed into the likeness of Christ, to become, as He is, divinely human, and thus to share His spiritual authority and charismatic power in the world.[78]

With the recovery of their true self, monks stand on their own feet by discovering their real but hidden identity in Christ, in which their spirit and God's Spirit become one.[79] As they awaken to the mystery of the presence of God, and increasingly live in this presence, they accelerate their maturity as sons and daughters of the Father. They have not attained final integration, but they are awake and aware of their shortcomings and strive to overcome them. They seek wholeness by pursuing integration of their

78. Merton, *Inner Experience*, 38.

79. Merton, *Inner Experience*, 38.

bodies, minds, and spirits, subjecting themselves to the Spirit of God, which enables openness to all persons of cultural and religious diversity and love for the family of humankind. They hope for a final and complete integration through full union with the Divine—conscious within Consciousness—realized within Reality—heaven—where they will experience the deepest aspiration of a monk, to stand on his or her own feet before God and see him, face to Face.

10

A Path to Peace

Thomas Merton, Final Integration, and Us[1]

IN TIMES OF GLOBAL disunity, conflict, and war, like we now face, Thomas Merton reveals that our communal path to peace relies on our individual integrative growth. He writes,

> At the root of all war is fear: not so much the fear men have of one another as the fear they have of everything. It is not merely that they do not trust one another; they do not even trust themselves . . . It is not only our hatred of others that is dangerous but also and above all our hatred of ourselves: particularly that hatred of ourselves which is too deep and too powerful to be consciously faced. For it is this which makes us see our own evil in others and unable to see it in ourselves. . . . For only love—which means humility—can exorcize the fear that is at the root of all war. . . . So instead of loving what you think is peace, love other men and love God above all. And instead of hating the people you think are warmakers, hate

---

1. Originally published in *Merton Seasonal*, 10–11.

the appetites and the disorder in your own soul, which
are the causes of war.[2]

Addressing this disorder in his soul, Merton's spiritual journey (undertaken not only for himself but us as well) was, in large measure, to realize growth through integration, which meant, for him, not only union with God and his neighbor, but also a degree of union with other cultures and religious traditions. Universal in outlook, Merton was "wide open to heaven and earth and closed to no one."[3] He worked toward this integration by embracing the totality of personhood—body, mind, and soul in union with the Spirit of God—with all of its creative potential as expressed in the humanities and art from varied cultures and spiritual traditions.

His initial breakthrough to God's love ripened so that toward the end of his life he became a mature lover, attaining to a "final integration . . . no longer limited by the culture in which he has grown up . . . retaining all that is best and most universal in them . . . giving birth to a fully comprehensive self . . . [which] accepts . . . all mankind."[4] Because we have the capacity to destroy both the earth and civilization, Merton insists, "whereas final . . . integration was, in the past, the privilege of a few, it is now becoming a need and aspiration of mankind as a whole."[5] He suggests that final integration should be a goal of everyone because the wholeness attained also becomes a path to societal peace and unity. For him, the fully integrated person promotes unity and peace among all.

For Merton, the great barrier to integration for individuals is the false self—the love we have for an illusionary self—which we project to the world and adore as an idol. He views the false self, the source of our self-hatred, as a series of accretions wound around the nothingness of a lie, and invites us to pierce its core through self-knowledge, contemplation, and grace. In doing so, with the light of faith, we discover our true self—a self in union

2. Merton. *New Seeds of Contemplation*, 112–22.

3. Merton, *Honorable Reader*, 112.

4. Merton, *Contemplation in a World of Action*, 212.

5. Merton, *Contemplation in a World of Action*, 216.

with the Spirit of God—and a special manifestation of Christ expressed through our individual personhood. We become a unique expression of the "one truth shining out in all its various manifestation," capable of bringing "perspective, liberty and spontaneity into the lives of others [as] a peacemaker."[6]

Merton summons us to find healing for this "disorder in our soul"[7] by embracing the Spirit of God, who will accelerate our own integration, and, through us, propel the integration of our communities. Thus, we may, like him, become a peacemaker, transcending the limitations of our culture and the barriers to peace. If, then, a critical mass of peacekeepers be achieved in any epoch, the dawn of a new age may be realized, fulfilling Isaiah's prophecy, "They shall beat their swords into plowshares, and their spears into pruning hooks: nation shall not lift up sword against nation, neither shall they learn war anymore."[8] Through the mercy of God, may we all begin the journey and make it so.

6. Merton, *Contemplation in a World of Action*, 212.

7. Merton, *New Seeds*, 122.

8. Isa 2:3–4.

11

The Road to Joy

A Circle Dance of Love, Thomas Merton, and the Pursuit of the True Self

FROM PRIMITIVE SOCIETIES TO modern times, when people gathered to dance, they often did so in a circle to mark special occasions and to celebrate community and togetherness. One thoughtful dancer suggested that as the dance goes into her life, everything becomes the dance. In the marrow of this circle of whirling flesh, as indeed in all of creation, there is the dance of life itself flowing from the Love of the Father for the Incarnate Son through the Spirit into creation and Love's return to the Father. All that exists pulsates in this great "Circle Dance of Love," which Thomas Merton characterized as the "cosmic dance," and to be in rhythm with it is to be on the road to joy.[1]

In this essay, we will travel Merton's *Road to Joy* by exploring his writings on the recovery of the true self, because for Merton it is the true self's communion with God that brings joy. As Thomas Merton wrote in *New Seeds of Contemplation*, "The only true joy on earth is to escape from the prison of our own false self, and

---

1. Merton, *New Seeds of Contemplation*, 25.

enter by love into union with the Life Who dwells and sings within the essence of every creature and in the core of our own souls."[2]

Traveling this road to joy, this essay explores from Merton's perspective the following questions: What is the false self? How do we recover our true self? What is the true self? Is the true self in union with God? What is the relationship of the true self to true joy?

WHAT IS THE FALSE SELF?

In *New Seeds of Contemplation*, Merton suggests,

> Every one of us is shadowed by an illusory person: a false self. This is the man that I want myself to be but who cannot exist, because God does not know anything about him. . . . And such a self cannot help but be an illusion. . . . Thus I use up my life in the desire for pleasures and the thirst for experiences, for power, honor, knowledge and love, to clothe this false self and construct its nothingness into something objectively real.[3]

At its core, this false self sees itself as a god. In *The Silent Life*, Merton suggests that "the inner, basic, metaphysical defilement of fallen man is his profound and illusory conviction that he is a god and that the universe is centered upon him."[4] This radical falsity births a selfhood that God does not know and, according to Merton, "that is altogether too much privacy."[5] This external mask creates a lens through which one falsely sees creation only in relationship to oneself. On this, Merton writes, "It is man's own technocratic and self-centered worldliness . . . which separates him from the reality of creation, and enables him to act out his fantasies as a little god, seeing and judging everything in relation to himself."[6]

---

2. Merton, *New Seeds of Contemplation*, 25.

3. Merton, *New Seeds of Contemplation*, 34.

4. Merton, *Silent Life*, 13–15.

5. Merton, *New Seeds of Contemplation*, 34.

6. Merton, *Conjectures of a Guilty Bystander*, 294.

For Merton, sin causes us to worship our false selves as an idol and estranges us from our true selves. As he writes, "When you think about what happens if our life is really dedicated to something other than God, then we are first of all alienated, and in a certain sense we are worshiping an idol."[7] Merton believes that sin and its effects also strike at the very depths of our personality by disrupting our orientation to God, the foundation of personhood and personality. He continues this point in *No Man Is an Island*, "Sin strikes at the very depth of our personality. It destroys the one reality on which our true character, identity, and happiness depend; our fundamental orientation to God."[8]

Merton existentially views this false self to be a pain of nonentity and nothingness, which leads to despair. He suggests that "the chronic inability to relax this cramp begets despair . . . we realize more and more that we are knotted upon nothing, that the cramp is a meaningless, senseless, pointless affirmation of nonentity . . . a makeshift identity which is nothing."[9] Man's no-to-everything and yes-to-himself orientation allows him to acquire such products of his will as wealth and power, forgoing the inner longings of his heart for love and the meaning of his life. For Merton, "He is as a god and therefore everything is within reach. But it turns out that all that he can successfully reach by his own volition is not quite worth having. What he really seeks and needs—love, an authentic identity, a life that has meaning—cannot be had merely by willing and by taking steps to procure them."[10]

What cannot be achieved by willing can be received as a gift if we are open to it. Merton insists, "In order to be open, we have to renounce ourselves, in a sense we have to die to our image of ourselves, our autonomy, our fixation upon our self-willed identity. We have to be able to relax the psychic and spiritual cramp which knots us in the painful, vulnerable, helpless 'I' that is all we know

7. Merton, *Thomas Merton in Alaska*, 76.
8. Merton, *No Man Is an Island*, 84.
9. Merton, *Conjectures of a Guilty Bystander*, 224.
10. Merton, *Conjectures of a Guilty Bystander*, 224.

as ourselves."[11] As we begin to relax this cramp, we must beware of distractions. In a world of overwhelming sensory barrages, Merton reminds us that these distractions suppress our discontent, delay the confronting of our false selves, and thereby delay facing our self-hate arising from the lie we make of our lives.

Similarly, in *The Monastic Journey*, Merton further unpacks the human struggle of confronting our false selves:

> What is it that makes every man struggle with himself? It is the deep, persistent voice of his own discontent with himself. . . . Distraction merely drowns out the inner voice. . . . And behind the smokescreen of amusements and projects, the inner dissatisfaction marshals all its forces for a more terrible assault when the distraction shall have been taken away. At last, the spirit that has fled from itself all its life, is stripped of its distractions at death and finds itself face to face with what can no longer be avoided; there is nothing now to prevent it from hating itself utterly, and totally, and forever.[12]

HOW DO WE RECOVER OUR TRUE SELF?

To recover our true selves, we must acknowledge the lie of the false self. Merton teaches that we have a choice of two identities: the external mask which seems to be real, and which lives by a shadowy autonomy for the brief moment of earthly existence and the hidden, inner person who seems to us to be nothing, but who can give themselves eternally to the truth in God.[13]

Our recovery depends on our cooperation with the Holy Spirit who, through the modalities of prayer, grace, silence, and solitude, leads us to our true self. We begin the journey with a commitment to a life of prayer. Merton believes prayer opens the door to self-knowledge, which allows the Holy Spirit to shine upon

11. Merton, *Conjectures of a Guilty Bystander*, 224.

12. Merton, *Monastic Journey*, 101.

13. Cunningham, *Thomas Merton*, 255.

the alleyways of our darkened interior.[14] A life of prayer leads us to our center, where we can experience the mercy of God,[15] and to union with God as well as communion with others.[16] This communion allows the community to touch God and God to touch the community. For Merton, "The mind that prays in me is more than my own mind, and the thoughts that come up in me are more than my own thoughts because this deep consciousness when I pray is a place of encounter between myself and God and between the common love of everybody."[17]

We continue the journey from the false self to the true self through grace. As Merton observed, "Once we find ourselves in the state of 'knowledge of good and evil' we have to accept the fact and understand our position, see it in relation to the innocence for which we were created, which we have lost and which we can regain."[18] Grace restores the innocence of our true self through the promptings of the Holy Spirit, our source of grace, our guide, and our destination. Realizing that the only source of the spiritual life is the Holy Spirit,[19] Merton believes grace prompts us to seek the truth of ourselves and our lives as we seek the truth that is God.

Through grace, we recover our true self through Christ's work in us, transforming us by shrouding himself with the wounds of our sins. As Merton argues, "The Christ we find in ourselves is not identified with what we vainly seek to admire and idolize in ourselves—on the contrary, He has identified himself with what we resent in ourselves, for He has taken upon Himself our wretchedness and our misery, our poverty and our sins."[20] By actualizing the recovery of our hidden identity in him, Christ transforms our self-hate into love, which promotes peace within us and thereby with others. Merton observes, "The peace which Christ brings is

14. Merton, *Thomas Merton in Alaska*, 160–61.

15. Merton, *Thomas Merton in Alaska*, 160.

16. Merton, *Thomas Merton in Alaska*, 136.

17. Merton, *Thomas Merton in Alaska*, 135.

18. Merton, *Zen and the Birds of Appetite*, 128.

19. Merton, *Contemplation in a World of Action*, 271.

20. Merton, *Monastic Journey*, 102.

the outcome of this war faced and fought on earth: man's war with himself, in which (by God's grace) he overcomes himself, conquers himself, pacifies himself, and can at last live with himself because he no longer hates himself."[21] Through the power of the Holy Spirit, grace liberates us from sin's creation of the false self.

Silence and solitude allow us to relax the psychic and spiritual cramp of our self, our "I," to immerse ourselves in the mystery of our identity in God. As Merton argues, "When we are quiet, not just for a few minutes, but for an hour or several hours, we may become uneasily aware of the presence within us of a disturbing stranger, the self that is both I and someone else."[22] Silence is healing since "silence makes us whole if we let it."[23] It helps us to concentrate on a purpose that really corresponds not only to the deeper needs of our own being but also to God's intentions for us.[24] Silence guides us to the solitude of our true self and the ground of our being, where we encounter God and peace. Merton thinks, "There is perfect peace, because we are grounded in infinite creative and redemptive Love. There we encounter God, whom no eye can see."[25] In this solitude, the inner door of one's heart opens, allowing the Spirit to flow and Love to be spoken.

In the journey to our true self, Merton cautions against particular ways or methods. Instead, he suggests we cultivate an attitude of openness. In unpacking this journey, James Finley writes of Merton's theology,

> Merton tells us that in seeking realization of our true self in prayer we should not look for a "method" or "system," but cultivate an "attitude," an "outlook": faith, openness, attention, reverence, expectation, supplication, trust, joy. All these finally permeate our being with love in so far as our living faith tells us we are in the presence of God, that we live in Christ, that in the Spirit of God we "see" God

21. Merton, *Monastic Journey*, 101.

22. Merton, *Essential Writings*, 74.

23. Merton, *Essential Writings*, 77.

24. Merton, *Essential Writings*, 77.

25. Merton, *Essential Writings*, 77.

our Father without "seeing." We know him in "unknowing." Faith is the bond that unites us to him in the Spirit who gives us light and love.[26]

Permeated by the Holy Spirit, prayer, grace, silence, and solitude will restore us to our true self.

WHAT IS THE TRUE SELF?

Merton believes our true self is our real but hidden identity in Christ. It is in Christ that our spirit and God's Spirit become one. This point of union is *le point vierge*, which is the hiding place of God within us, inaccessible to our meddling but realized by those who see God through grace and purity of heart. We acquire our identity in God, which is the true self's union with Christ. In Merton's view,

> The secret of my identity is hidden in the love and mercy of God. . . . Ultimately the only way that I can be myself is to become identified with Him in Whom is hidden the reason and fulfillment of my existence. Therefore, there is only one problem on which all my existence, my peace and my happiness depend: to discover myself in discovering God. If I find Him I will find myself and if I find my true self I will find Him.[27]

Our true self fosters a life of peace and union with others, in which communications become communion. Merton describes the true self in his epiphany at the intersection of Fourth and Walnut in Louisville, Kentucky: "At the center of our being is a point of nothingness which is untouched by sin and by illusion, a point of pure truth, a point or spark which belongs entirely to God . . . This little point of nothingness and of absolute poverty is the pure glory of God in us."[28]

26. Finley, *Merton's Palace of Nowhere*, 93.

27. Merton, *New Seeds of Contemplation*, 35.

28. Merton, *Conjectures of a Guilty Bystander*, 158.

IS THE TRUE SELF IN UNION WITH GOD?

From Merton's perspective, to recover the true self is to be in union with God. He believes the Spirit leads us to the core of our being and awakens us to our true identity in Christ.

But, in fact, the resurrection and ascension of Christ—the new Adam—completely restored human nature to its spiritual condition and made possible the divinization of every person coming into the world. This meant that, in each one of us, the inner self was now able to be awakened and transformed by the action of the Holy Spirit, and this awakening would not only enable us to discover our true identity "in Christ" but would also make the living and risen Savior present in us.[29]

Our true self is our identity in Christ, which is derived from the distinct unity of our personhood and the Spirit of Christ, such that Christ is living in us, and we are living in him. The effect of this union is that we become a new creation, a unique expression of Christ in the world. Grounded in Christ, we are in communion with others by sharing the same center, his Spirit. Hence the love we receive from the indwelling Christ flows out to others as we receive their love in return. Merton explains this thusly,

> The union of the Christian with Christ is not just a similarity of inclination and feeling, a mutual consent of minds and wills. It has a more radical, more mysterious and supernatural quality: it is a mystical union in which Christ Himself becomes the source and principle of divine life in me. . . . We receive Him in the "inspiration" of secret love, and we give Him to others in the outgoing of our own charity. Our life in Christ is then a life both of receiving and of giving. We receive from God, in the Spirit, and in the same Spirit we return our love to God through our brothers.[30]

The Holy Spirit then helps us grow in our love of our neighbor by deepening the realization of this communion with ourselves,

29. Merton, *Inner Experience*, 38.

30. Merton, *New Seeds of Contemplation*, 158.

each other, and Christ. Merton expressed the depths of this communion in one of his last utterances before he died:

> And the deepest level of communication is not communication, but communion. It is wordless. It is beyond words, and it is beyond speech, and is beyond concept. Not that we discover a new unity. We discover an older unity. My dear brothers, we are already one. But we imagine that we are not. What we have to recover is our original unity. What we have to be is what we are.[31]

WHAT IS THE RELATIONSHIP OF THE TRUE SELF TO TRUE JOY?

Merton teaches us that true joy arises from the recovery of our true self, which is the image and likeness of Christ. In his view, Christ-centered persons are capable of true joy because they, like Christ, will what God wills. Merton elaborates, "True joy is found in the perfect willing of what we were made to will: in the intense and supple and free movement of our will rejoicing in what is good not merely for us but in Itself."[32] For Merton, the origin of this gift of joy stems from the incarnation of Christ. In *Conjectures of a Guilty Bystander*, he writes, "I have the immense joy of being man, a member of a race in which God himself became incarnate."[33] Christ's gift by the outpouring of the Holy Spirit through his death and resurrection facilitates the recovery of our true self and thereby restores us to a realized "image and likeness of God." This image and likeness of God is the mysterious indwelling of Christ that permeates our personhood.

Our union with God through the true self's identity in Christ is an encounter with Love, the dynamic flow of God's energy. This indwelling Love is the source of our capacity to more fully obey the commandment of Christ to love God *and* our neighbor. By

31. Merton, *Asian Journal*, 308.

32. Merton, *New Seeds of Contemplation*, 259–60.

33. Merton, *Conjectures of a Guilty Bystander*, 157.

following the ways of this love, one grows in the realization of Christ's promise in John, "That my joy may be in you and that your joy may be complete."[34] This is a joy tied to the love of others. As Christ instructs us,

> As the Father has loved me, so have I loved you. Now remain in my love. If you keep my commands, you will remain in my love, just as I have kept my Father's commands and remain in his love. I have told you this so that my joy may be in you and that your joy may be complete. My command is this: Love each other as I have loved you.[35]

Hence, for our joy to be complete we must remain in his Love. To remain in his Love, we must forever deepen our union with him by our true self more completely embracing our identity in Christ. Through this embrace we radiate love to others and receive their love in return. On this, Merton observes, "One of the paradoxes of the mystical life is this: that a man cannot enter into the deepest center of himself and pass through that center into God, unless he is able to pass entirely out of himself and empty himself and give himself to other people in the purity of a selfless love."[36]

Animated by the loving energy radiating from our union with God, we consciously join this "Circle Dance of Love" flowing from the Father through the Son-as-Spirit into creation. A dance Merton knew well. In *New Seeds of Contemplation*, he writes,

> The Lord plays and diverts Himself in the garden of His creation, and if we could let go of our own obsession with what we think is the meaning of it all, we might be able to hear His call and follow Him in His mysterious, cosmic dance . . . The world and time are the dance of the Lord in emptiness. The silence of the spheres is the music of a wedding feast . . . Indeed we are in the midst of it, and it is in the midst of us, for it beats in our very blood, whether we want it to or not. Yet the fact remains that we

34. John 15:11.

35. John 15:11–14.

36. Merton, *New Seeds of Contemplation*, 64.

are invited to forget ourselves on purpose, cast our awful solemnity to the winds and join in the general dance.[37]

Thomas Merton danced along this road to joy and beckons us to follow. He summons us to pursue the recovery of our true self, working toward our liberation and birth into true joy. If we travel that road, he suggests we will realize our true self's identity in Christ—the source of our ability to keep Christ's command to remain in his Love so that our joy may be complete. Merton guides us as a partner in this cosmic dance where incarnational love burns the coals of our false self and erupts as a living flame from the embers of our true self's identity in Christ. If we embrace our identity, we will radiate God's Love to others and receive their Love in return. Doing so completes this circle dance by fueling an ever-more intense communal flame of love. In this circle dance of love, the Spirit of Christ is the road to joy, the creator of joy, and, in Itself, the very dance of joy.

37. Merton, *New Seeds of Contemplation*, 296–97.

12

A Stranger No More

An automobile accident disrupts my planned presentation at the "Seventh General Meeting of The Thomas Merton Society Meeting of Great Britain and Ireland." Pondering the writings of Albert Camus and Thomas Merton during my hospitalization and recovery gave a deeper appreciation for the conference's theme, "The Voice of the Stranger." In the course of this unplanned journey, I reflect on the question, *Who is the stranger?* I realize. The stranger is a person I do not know. The stranger is someone I am when I am in a foreign place. The stranger is the false self I created whom God does not know. The stranger is Christ whose Spirit and my true self become one Spirit, making me and others strangers no more.

The stranger is a person I do not know.

Shuddering in the cold on a mountain top, I await sunrise with my family. The sun rises beneath us with its warmth and beauty as we stand on Mount Sinai where Moses witnessed the glory of God. The trip is ordinary in every way—except for the camel ride to the foot of the steep climb to the summit and the Bedouin stranger who escorts me arm-in-arm to the peak, extolling, "We have one Father." On Mount Sinai and in my encounter with this stranger, I reflect on Merton's proclamation, "God speaks, and God is to be heard, not only on Sinai, not only in my own heart but in the voice of the stranger . . . God must be allowed the right to speak unpredictably."[1] And he does so.

Two weeks later I am hospitalized in a trauma intensive care unit from an automobile accident. Surrounded by strangers, I am totally dependent on them to tend to my body as I lie helpless, stripped physically, mentally, and emotionally. Through the care of these strangers, God speaks a message of care and love.

The stranger is someone I am when in a foreign place.

A foreigner and stranger, I stand at Jethro's well in Saint Catherine's monastery on the Sinai Peninsula where, several thousand years earlier, Moses met his future wife and perceived himself a stranger: "So Moses settled with this man who gave him his daughter Zipporah in marriage. She gave him a son and he named him Gershom, because he said, 'I am a stranger in a foreign land.'"[2] Here, too, the Israelites trekked with Moses as foreigners. We, like the wandering Israelites, remain estranged from God until we, through our interior journey, awake to the realization of his indwelling presence within us. We begin our journey when we confront our false selves.

The stranger is the false self I created whom God does not know.

In his literary essays, Thomas Merton reflects on the works of the writer and existentialist philosopher Albert Camus and provides insight into the false self that God does not know, as man is alienated from his true self, which is made in the image and likeness of God. Such a person appears in Camus's *The Stranger*. Camus chronicles the interior life of someone devoid of a meaningful encounter with another human being, much less God. However, through the protagonist, Meursault, we discover that his false self is akin to ours and that we are brothers in our alienation from our true selves. Children of Adam and Eve, we all inherit the seeds of falsity that make us strangers in exile from our true selves. On the

1. Merton, "Letter to Pablo Antonia Cuadra," 384.
2. Exod 2:19, 21–22 (NJB).

one hand, Camus correctly perceives this situation of man as absurd; on the other, Merton encourages us to acknowledge our false selves, seek our true self, and thereby become strangers no more.

Meursault lives an alienated and isolated life with a selfhood that God does not know. The plot of this novel is that Meursault, casually and almost by happenstance, kills another man and is metaphorically convicted more for not crying at his mother's funeral than for committing murder. His detachment and indifference convict him in the eyes of society. The prosecutor sums up his case not with the act of murder but with Meursault's behavior at his mother's funeral, "Gentlemen of the jury, the day after his mother's death, this man was out swimming, starting up a dubious liaison, and going to the movies, a comedy, for laughs. I have nothing further to say."[3]

Camus quickly thrusts us into his character's detachment and poverty from the first sentence of the novel, which relates Meursault's emphasis on the details of a telegram announcing his mother's death rather than an emotional response to his loss. Meursault's ruminations and behavior outline the poverty of his relationships. He does not seemingly love his mother or his girlfriend. Having witnessed an acquaintance beat a girlfriend, he promises to support him with the police. He also agrees to write a letter for him to seduce the girlfriend into returning for the purpose of continuing the abuse. Meursault realizes that he has killed a man only after the police interrogation. He feels like a spectator at his own trial and at times forgets that it is *his* trial, weighing the pros and cons of the arguments as though he were a member of the audience. Even his girlfriend testifies to Meursault's emotional detachment after his mother's death, describing the activities of their time together.

In his analysis of Camus's *The Stranger*, Thomas Merton points to Meursault's passivity in remaining in his poverty even though society is ultimately responsible for it. He writes,

> The poverty of Meursault is the product of a social system which needs people to be as he is and therefore manufactures them in quantity—and condemns them for being

3. Schofer, "Rhetoric of the Text," 143.

> what they are . . . Meursault remained in his poverty, his
> absurd, solipsistic loneliness. He was not able to find and
> integrate himself completely by compassion and solidar-
> ity with others who, like himself, were poor.[4]

Merton believes that "the stranger is an ironic study in extreme
poverty, the man who has no interiority, who does nothing, makes
no choice, has no real purpose, cannot be justified, has not God;
even his crime is not really his—it is so automatic, so mechanical."[5]
His crime was almost accidental. He happened to be on the beach;
the Arab, his victim, happened to be there. It was as though nature
fired the shot through him:

> It seemed to me as if the sky split open from one end to
> the other to rain down fire. My whole being tensed and I
> squeezed my hand around the revolver. The trigger gave;
> I felt the smooth underside of the butt; and there, in that
> noise, sharp and deafening at the same time, is where it
> all started. . . . Then I fired four more times at the mo-
> tionless body where the bullets lodged without leaving a
> trace. And it was like knocking four quick times on the
> door of unhappiness.[6]

Commenting on the murder, Merton observes, "The murder
is the fruit of this passive, automatic existence—and an awakening
from it. The shooting is almost entirely an accident. Completely
unmotivated, it occurs under the blazing noonday sun of North
Africa in a trance of acedia worthy of a desert father."[7] As his writing indicates, Camus perceives Meursault as a man of integrity
whose situation is absurd. His integrity arises from his authenticity. "He is a man poor and naked," who "refuses every mask," who
"refuses to lie . . . by saying more than he feels . . . in love with
the sun that casts no shadows," and animated "by profound passion . . . for the absolute and for truth."[8] Meursault's authenticity

4. Merton, "Stranger," 301.

5. Merton, "Stranger," 292.

6. Camus, *Stranger*, 59.

7. Merton, "Stranger," 294.

8. Merton, "Stranger," 298.

relates to the congruence of his expressions and feelings within his capacity to perceive them. His passion for the absolute and the truth is limited to the absolute and the truth which he can know.

Camus strips his character Meursault of illusions about himself and starkly portrays his selfhood as unconnected to those around him, while revealing the depth of Meursault's interior poverty as well as his poverty of relationships. Through this character, Camus provides a mirror in which we can view our own false selves. Our own selfhood is a lens through which we can view ourselves and others. Our capacity to see accurately depends on the clarity of this lens. The more opaque our selfhood becomes through its falsity, the more it obscures our ability to know, relate, and love ourselves and others. In regard to Meursault's passion for the absolute and the truth, the falsity of his selfhood limits and taints his capacity to seek the absolute and the truth, which exist irrespective of Camus's and Meursault's ability to perceive them. Meursault's selfhood becomes an island isolated both from his true self, who could perceive the absolute and the truth, and the true selves of others. Camus uses the term *absurd* to communicate this sense of the stranger's isolation and alienation. Camus explains the origin of this feeling of the absurd,

> A world that can be explained even with bad reasons is a familiar world. But, on the other hand, in a universe suddenly divested of illusions and light man feels an alien, a stranger. His exile is without remedy since he is deprived of a memory of a lost home or the hope of a promised land. This divorce between man and his life, the actor and his setting, is properly the feeling of the absurd.[9]

Although Meursault recognizes the absurdity of society and refuses to play its game, he fails to recognize both his own absurdity and the stranger within himself. His true poverty results from his lack of love, which underlies his passivity, indifference, and detachment. Reflecting on Camus's idea of the absurd, Merton writes of Meursault,

9. Camus, *Myth of Sisyphus*, 13.

One gives life a meaning by living it in openness and solidarity with others. But Meursault is utterly impoverished because he is utterly alone. He is caught in his own absurdity because having rightly rejected the hypocrisy of systematic answers and explanations proposed by others, he has not entered into solidarity with anyone else. He does not love anyone else. He does not love Marie, or his mother, or his neighbors, or his friends.[10]

It is his failure to love that makes Meursault a stranger to himself. Camus demonstrates Meursault's indifference and self-centeredness while maintaining his emotional honesty in this playful exchange between Meursault and Marie, his girlfriend: "She was wearing a pair of my pajamas with the sleeves rolled up. When she laughed I wanted her again. A minute later she asked me if I loved her. I told her it didn't mean anything but that I didn't think so. She looked sad. But as we were fixing lunch, and for no apparent reason, she laughed in such a way that I kissed her."[11]

Meursault permanently excludes the possibility of love by his disbelief in repentance and redemption. He willfully excludes the option of transcending his alienated selfhood in a moment of rage triggered by the prison chaplain's bothersome questions. Meursault comments, "The chaplain knew the game well too, I could tell right away: his gaze never faltered. And his voice didn't falter, either, when he said, 'Have you no hope at all? And do you really live with the thought that when you die, you die, and nothing remains?' 'Yes,' I said."[12]

Rejecting the entreaties of the prison priest, Meursault erupts into rage directed at the chaplain, and that rage results in his epiphany. In awakening to the world's indifference, Meursault forgoes the possibility of love and hope and has only the wish to experience the mob's hate at his execution.

> As if that blind rage has washed me clean, rid me of
> hope; for the first time, that night alive with signs and

10. Merton, "Stranger," 299.

11. Camus, *Stranger*, 35.

12. Camus, *Stranger*, 117.

> stars, I opened myself to the gentle indifference of the
> world. Finding it so much like myself—so like a brother,
> really—I felt that I had been happy and that I was happy
> again. For everything to be consummated, for me to feel
> less alone, I had only to wish that there be a large crowd
> of spectators the day of my execution and that they greet
> me with cries of hate.[13]

By his fixed and arrested interior development, Meursault *chooses* alienation over love. This is his true prison, making him a stranger to others as well as to himself. It is also ours. To escape this prison, we must take a journey which Meursault refuses to make. We must abandon our false selves in search of our true selves, which is made in the image and likeness of God. It is the false self, through an estrangement with the true self, that is the stranger within us whom God does not know and the stranger we make of each other. In Merton's words,

> Every one of us is shadowed by a false self. This is the
> [person] I want myself to be but who cannot exist, be-
> cause God does not know anything about him. And to
> be unknown to God is altogether too much privacy. My
> false and private self is the one who wants to exist outside
> the reach of God's will and God's love—outside of reality
> and outside of life. And such a self cannot help but be an
> illusion.[14]

Such is the false selfhood of Meursault—an illusion outside of God's love and outside of life—who serves as a lesson to us all.

Those on their journey to their true selves must acknowledge this interior stranger. Merton observes, "In returning to God and to ourselves, we have to begin with what we actually are. We have to start from our alienated condition. We are prodigals in a distant country, 'the region of unlikeness,' and we travel far in that region before we seem to reach our own land (and yet secretly we are in our own land all the time!)."[15]

13. Camus, *Stranger*, 122–23.

14. Merton, *New Seeds of Contemplation*, 33.

15. Merton, *New Seeds of Contemplation*, 280–81.

The stranger, in one of his disguises, is Christ whose Spirit and my true self become one Spirit, making me and the other strangers no more.

To recognize Christ in the stranger we must first pass through the stranger within ourselves. I can identify with Meursault by finding aspects of his selfhood within myself. In a more hedonistic phase of my life, I experienced the detachment, indifference, and subsequent alienation arising from a self-centeredness that caused a rift between me and my life. I found that at the end of this path was not only a sense of the absurd but also despair. With the aid of grace, I attempted to trace the roots of this selfhood that was incapable of love. I discovered that it originated in an impulse to make a god of myself that nurtures a fabricated self built upon drives to lust, power, and wealth. The aim of this self is not to love but to control and dominate, to be admired and worshiped. I share with Meursault a false selfhood which is detached, alienated, and unloving. It has its roots in the mysterious consequences of Adam and Eve's choice to be like God. Camus appears to me to be correct. Our situation is absurd because our self-centeredness imprisons us within a falsity, which is divorced from life and disconnected from our own context. However, there is another self, hidden within us, the one through which we love. There is a true self made in the image and likeness of God, which bathes in the light of the indwelling presence of God that lives in us. Paradoxically, the false self strives to make itself a god, whereas the true self is, through mystery, co-joined with God.

Merton shows us the way out of our falsity when he writes, "A man cannot enter into the deepest center of himself and pass through that center into God unless he is able to pass entirely out of himself and empty himself and give himself to other people in the purity of selfless love."[16]

For Merton, spirituality was precisely this journey from the false self to the true self. It is a journey to God that passes through the heart of the stranger and engages the stranger within. It is a gift of grace for the seeker, with a parched thirst, to see the face of the

16. Merton, *New Seeds of Contemplation*, 64.

living God. This thirst leads him into the warrens and caverns of his own interior with its attachments, delusions, and the ferocity of its desires. Slow progress is made by one's efforts. Growth occurs with the help of the Spirit. Saint John of the Cross describes this process in the *Dark Night of the Soul* and in the *Living Flame of Love*. Like a log of wood burnt by fire, the soul is slowly purified by the Spirit until it becomes a living flame itself. For, unlike Meursault, who forsook hope, love, and life after death based on beliefs that excluded repentance and redemption, Saint John's person embraces hope, love, and life after death based on an encounter with this spiritual fire.

We are destined for an encounter with an incomprehensible living God whose nature is love. It is a love without boundaries. This redemptive love allows a Son to make himself a sacrifice and be nailed to a cross. It is, in the end, a love that is unexplainable. Nor are we asked to explain it, but rather to live in it. That is the goal of the contemplative journey—to realize that tiny spark at the core of our being, which is love itself, where his Being and our being are one. Merton offers us insight into this relationship, "If the deepest ground of my being is love, then in that very love itself and nowhere else will I find myself, and the world, and my brother [and sister] in Christ. It is not a question of either/or—but of all in one . . . of wholeness, wholeheartedness and unity . . . which finds the same ground of love in everything."[17] Our true self is in union with love for which there are no strangers—either within or without. *To know that love as the center of one's being is to know the center of all beings.* With this knowledge, the other is a stranger no more.

Merton witnesses the union of our true selves and God's Spirit when he writes,

> The contemplative has nothing to tell you except to reassure you and say that, if you dare to penetrate your own silence and risk the sharing of that solitude with the lonely other who seeks God through you, then you will truly recover the light and the capacity to understand

17. Merton, *Contemplation in a World of Action*, 155–56.

> what is beyond words and beyond explanations because
> it is too close to be explained: it is the intimate union, in
> the depths of your own heart, of God's spirit and your
> own secret inmost self, so that you and [God] are in all
> truth One Spirit.[18]

From these insights and his own life journey, Merton grasps the realization that someone may be a stranger to himself and others, as a false self divorced from his true self, but concludes that, in the reality of our existence in God, there are no strangers. As one of his last testaments before his death, he proclaimed that we have to become what we already are—we are already *one*. When we awaken to this realization, we come to recognize that the other-as-a-stranger is Christ in one of his disguises. When we journey beyond the stranger within ourselves, whom God does not know, we discover that Christ's spirit dwells within us, making us and the other strangers no more.

Juxtaposing my exterior ascent of Mount Sinai and my interior descent during my hospitalization, I experience my own alienation from my true self as I recall a young boy racing after me near the great pyramids of Egypt pleading for me to buy his postcards. Even after I stepped into the van, he ran alongside, his face contorted into an anguished plea. His desperation was more about survival than peddling. I am awake all night accused by the flame of my conscience of my rich American indifference to the cry of the poor. There remains incompleteness in me, in my world: the unmet cry of the poor, the stranger in the boy racing along the van, the cry of Meursault, the cry of those who care for me in the hospital.

There are those to whom I am still a stranger and who indict me as a stranger to myself. Yet amid my brokenness, in the distance of my interior, I hear faintly a plea from the unborn Christ—the ultimate stranger—to me and to you, the innkeepers of the world, *"Please don't shut me out!"*

18. Merton, *Hidden Ground of Love*, 158.

13

Reflections

Grow Foolish in Love[1]

UNCLE AFIF, MY MOTHER's brother from Lebanon, came and went. He flew into Birmingham from Washington, DC, one Sunday and off to Beirut on Thursday.

I had met him once, fourteen years before, in Beirut. For Lebanon it was a quiet time with little portent of what was to come. Then, their society seemed to me to have a controlled chaos, mirrored in their wild driving, their bazaars, their restlessness. Yet, they demonstrated great hospitality. They were generous, took time for one another, valued leisure and friendship.

In 1982, my uncle came to visit me in Birmingham. He watched television, played with my oldest son, John, and bought him a Smurf riding toy, pushing him up and down the driveway. He had lunch with two priests and went to daily Mass.

The two of us went to New Orleans, had breakfast at Brennan's, where we waited an hour for a table. He had his portrait made (a portrait he nicknamed "Himself" and gave to my mother). We took a cruise around the Mississippi River, went up the trade

---

1. This reflection was written in 1982 after the visit of Uncle Afif to Birmingham.

market building for the view, and walked down Bourbon Street. He bought gifts, prayer beads and a lighter for me, a gold medallion for my wife (although he bought a frame for it in New Orleans, he couldn't resist noting that "prices were cheaper" in Lebanon).

As I visited with him, he gradually began to share his interior self. His words were always polite and charming—always kind and gentle. Yet he was very strong—he stood on his own feet—not easily swayed by events or opinions. In him lived the spirits of his father and his brothers. His personality included the story-telling talent of his father; the strength and persuasiveness of his brother Chafic; the cherubic features of his brother Chakeeb; the intellect of his older brother Jad; and the charm of his brother Chahin; all of whom were dead. I was particularly impressed by his openness and warmth, his spontaneity and joy in living. He appeared to be a passionate man.

Gradually, I came to see that at the core of his interior was the flame of a lover, who loved himself, his neighbor, the world, and God. He took care of himself, watched his diet, though he enjoyed food and fine clothes, but in simplicity and good taste. He loved to immerse himself in the reality of creation and created things. It seemed to me that he had erased much of the distinction between what we label good or bad by choosing to love his neighbor and his world. One evening we went to Mass and dinner—afterward he suggested a show on Bourbon Street. I teased him, "Should we go to a show after Mass?"

He said we could do both! However, we didn't go. After seeing Bourbon Street and peeking through the doors, he thought the shows were cheap and definitely not for families! Apparently, he was thinking of something else, perhaps a cabaret. He appeared very relaxed with the sexuality around him and communicated a joyful innocence and purity in his appreciation of beauty.

This, too, is the man who told me, while we were high up in the chic, revolving Top of the Mart lounge perched on New Orleans' World Trade Center, that people are too selfish, seeking wealth and pleasure. There, too, he said that the poor (he was secretary of the Saint Vincent de Paul Society in Lebanon) need the gift of our touch in addition to material things. He went each week into their war-torn homes. He raised money on their behalf and gave them something more precious—himself. As the Top of Mart revolved, creating the illusion of the lights of New Orleans turning before us, he took advantage of the analogy to explain our relationship to God. He said what God sees is real, and in us there is much illusion, and in our relationship with God our illusions were the source of much error and unhappiness. A man tries to be and do what God created him for. He never knows for sure that he is doing it. But he tries. He does what he can.

Finally, in his characteristic earnestness, he gathered himself enthusiastically, yet fumbling for the English words to express himself, to declare, as our five days together drew to a close, and we began the process of physically and emotionally separating our tight and newly formed bond, "To love is to become foolish—the more we love the more foolish we are."

So, what does he and his visit mean to me? He brought me a spark—a tiny, strong spark of love—a spark that has survived the massacres, the bombings, the rubble, the chaos, and the terror ongoing in Lebanon. He has brought me a cutting from the Lebanese cedars to plant in my heart, for it to take root and grow. He watered and nurtured it with sayings and heritage. He connected me to my ancestral roots—he gave me a history and a place.

As a son of Lebanon, I go back to the dawn of civilization—I am a son of man and of God—I have a covenant. I am one more offshoot of the beloved cedars of Lebanon, which are sacred trees and consecrated signs of the Most High God. In me, there is a promise to "grow foolish in love."

Afterword

Dad and I originally discussed this book project when he was first diagnosed with cancer in the fall of 2016. We were all concerned about the lymphoma, with a murky, but not dismal, prognosis. My brothers and I, his only daughter, made several trips home over that fall and into winter to take him to his various appointments and the botanical gardens, where he loved to walk and where he took us when we were children. We mostly came to spend time with him. After the chemotherapy treatment was successful and Dad entered remission in January 2017, we said we would get to the book when we had more time. At that point, one brother was in a Carmelite monastery studying to become a priest, another brother was buying and renovating his first home and getting ready to start a family, and I was finishing my doctorate and getting ready to move out West with my partner. Winter turned to summer, summer to fall, when we learned that dad's symptoms of extreme itchiness and weight loss were indicative of stage four liver cancer. He had, we were told by the medical staff, months if we were lucky, weeks if not. Then there wasn't time to talk about the book. There were clinical trials to comb through and try to get into, there were affairs to get in order, there was precious time needed to be spent together doing the kinds of things we liked to do as a family, a walk in the gardens, a dinner with friends. Dad died seven weeks after his second cancer diagnosis.

The themes that animate this book, *his* book, are the same principles he lived throughout his life—caritas, love, communion with all things, caring for one another, and a recognition that it is through our brokenness that we inch closer to God. These are the ideas he exercised daily as he searched for the healing spirit—that spirit that guides us, lifts us up, holds us together—on the road to joy. And it is in this spirit that I sought to write the following during his death.

We watch the game. As we've always done. At least as long as I can remember. Dad, hoarse, screams for the boys of Notre Dame to get first downs, make big and small plays. They come from behind to best LSU on an incredible last play. We scream. I'm standing and hollering. It *is* an incredible play. I wonder if this is the last Notre Dame football game he will ever watch. I want them to win it for him, and I notice that I am thinking a lot about lasts. Like last summer when I was moving from New Orleans, where I did my doctorate, to Sacramento, where I have just recently gotten a tenure-track job. I thought a lot about lasts then too. Thoughts refracted through activities. Is it my last time going to Pizza D, my favorite pizza place? Or my last time going for an impromptu Tuesday night in the French Quarter with friends? Or the last time I would go to Pagoda, my neighborhood coffee shop?

Thinking, obsessing, and imagining loss before it happens. One of the particulars about life, generally, and loss, specifically, is the jumbling of time—past, present, future, pluperfect—and space. And this jumble itself becoming a place that is a song in and of itself and one I've traversed many times. Dad and I can't believe they won; glad they pulled it off at the end. I realize that he might not be so preoccupied with lasts as I. That maybe his accounting of time is one different from mine.

I sit here. I sit here, as he lays dying, and it is not how I thought it would be. I think about our last real hug. About the casual way we said good night—how we always said good night, with heartfelt hugs and I love yous. And what I realize, in this instant, is that I am not so concerned with lasts. It's not the lasts, not with him, but it's every single moment. I do not analyze and re-evaluate the last time we hugged, or the last time we disagreed, or the last time I was frustrated with him. I am filled with every hug and every I love you and memories I had forgotten I had. I am filled with the day-to-day of the everyday. Ordinary meals on the porch at home, his favorite place. Conversations ranging from my grades to world politics to theology to how I felt. Firsts. Lasts. They don't matter now. Only all things between. Every single hello, every single argument, every single laugh, every single incantation of his voice. I am left with all the moments, big and small, forever grateful for the time we had.

At Dad's appointment for an ultrasound, the day after his surprising liver cancer diagnosis, when we don't yet know what it means but feel it is something awful, we go to the Original Pancake House, and he says, "What I'm facing here is death." He asks me to take care of my mom, he says he wants me to have a closer relationship with God. He says he is a contemplative, has been since his father died, communing daily with God, who he thinks of as a living energy of love. I look out the window. Out a window I have looked through so many times—since I was a kid and we came here for brunch on the weekends; as a teenager with friends to discuss the existentialisms of the day and to get away from our parents; as a college student, home and catching up with those same friends—I hold back the tears his words summon. I fight to stay in this moment, to be with him as we both realize what this diagnosis means. I tell him about my God. About how I find God in the moments when someone offers kindness when you need it most. And he says that's right. I say I find God in my community, in being with people and being present *in* the present with them. He nods. I tell him he doesn't need to worry about us. That we are all okay. Better than okay, that we are healthy and happy and contribute meaningfully to society. That we live with the principles he has taught us, to recognize and fight injustice, to be good to others, to make time for family and friends, to live with *tenderheartedness*.

It was the kind of conversation that only happens occasionally and if we are very lucky and work hard to connect to one another.

The palliative care and comfort unit has its own orchestra of sounds. There is a constant drip that sounds like an aquarium. That's the oxygen. There's a low hum that alternates its tones, like a very miniature roller coaster coaxing its way up, against gravity, and back down again. That's the titration machine. As healthcare incessantly modernizes in its quest for health, I wonder which aspects of the present modernity thwart or foster the caritas he sought to make the animating force of the healthcare system. Dad's wristband has a barcode; all the orders have barcodes, the antibiotic, the pain medicine, the IV. A digital record. One brother prays. Another brother writes. Maybe a eulogy. Maybe a letter. The sounds give me a sense of the world, the one that surrounds us, ripples through us, and leaves us on the other side, with the greatest light. As Dad wrote nearly a half century ago,

> *A polished mirror reflects great light;*
> *a broken mirror generates even more;*
> *the greatest light arises from no mirror, no light—just this!*

Three Saturdays ago, I sat with Dad in the kitchen. He answered the phone, heard Mary say her birthday was on the ninth. He asked what kind of cake she wanted. Three days later he would take her to lunch and shopping for groceries. Dad and I talked about what electronics to get my brother before he returned to his studies the following week. We went for a walk in the gardens with Mom. We watched a movie. Two Saturdays ago, I waited in the hospital room in the palliative care unit for my father to stop breathing. Between one Saturday and the next, following small steps along the road to joy and a final charitable act, Dad was admitted to the palliative care unit. We thought with fluids and antibiotics he might get to go home to hospice. I am in the room alone. Dad has not been responsive for maybe a day. I talk to him in case he can hear me. I talk to him because he is my dad and I want him to know how much I love him and how much I miss him and that I will take care of everything. But he knows all of this already. We wait for him to stop breathing. We wait a week. Then he stops. Last Saturday, I, with my family, planned Dad's funeral and visitation. I stop by the funeral home to drop off the shirt and tie that mom and I want him to be buried in. To discuss final details. Today, Saturday, is Dad's birthday. We ask friends and family to do a random act of kindness in Dad's honor for his birthday—the first without him.

I am standing on a hill in Northern California overlooking Lake Berryessa. It's been a rocky ascent and I am tired and sore. It is beautiful. My father will never see this lake, not like we had planned a few months ago. Death also liberates time for the living. I think Dad has already seen this lake, will have seen it, is seeing it; that to be dead is another way of saying that we no longer experience time through our finitude but rather through infinitudes. That we know time (as all things will be known) as it is and not as we experience it to be. I recall the many theological and philosophical conversations Dad and I had about God and eternal time and his concept of what it is and I offered my best post-structuralist, seminary-infused theology of something like a spirituality of quantum physics. I remember agreeing more than disagreeing and always arriving at the same place by different means. I am comforted in thinking that Dad exists beyond our experience. I like imagining that Dad is everywhere and nowhere. That all that has been and all that is to come is safely in his grasp. I enjoy imagining him mingling with the saints and all those who came before and will come long after we're gone. It makes me think of a poem I jotted down years ago and that he loved:

> *it's nice*
> *being here*
> *with you*
> *watching*
> *the clouds*
> *to see*
> *if*
> *it will pour*
> *or*
> *roll on by.*

Afterword

waiting
together
to see what'll happen.

Clare E. B. Cannon
Across infinite spacetime
Sacramento, California

Bibliography

Allchin, Arthur. "Thomas Merton and the Christian East." In *Merton and Hesychasm: The Prayer of the Heart,* edited by Bernadette Dieker and Jonathan Montaldo. Louisville: Fons Vitae, 2003.

Augustine. *The Confessions.* Westmont, IL: Clark, 1876.

Bessenecker, Scott A. *The New Friars.* Downers Grove: InterVarsity Press, 2006.

Bonhoeffer, Deitrich. *Life Together.* San Francisco: Harper & Row, 1954.

———. *A Testament to Freedom.* San Francisco: HarperCollins, 1995.

Camus, Albert. *The Myth of Sisyphus.* Translated by Justin O'Brien. Harmondsworth, UK: Penguin, 1975.

———. *The Stranger.* Translated by Mathew Ward. New York: Vintage International, 1989.

Cannon, Nassif J. "The Broken Healer." *Humane Medicine* 3 (1987) 121–23.

———. "The Broken Healer: If They Do Not Remain Whole, How Can They Heal?" In *Educating the Christian Doctor,* by Edmund D. Pellegrino et al., 35–42. CMDS Study Guide Series. 1989.

———. "How Tender Our Wounds: A Meditation on Competence in Caring." *Humane Medicine* 8 (1992) 231–37.

———."A Path to Peace—Thomas Merton, Final Integration, and Us." *Merton Seasonal* 40 (2015), 10–11.

———. "A Quest for Health." In *Caring from the Heart: The Convergence of Caring and Spirituality,* edited by Simone Roach, 28–44. New York: Paulist, 1997.

———. "Stand on Your Own Feet! Thomas Merton and the Monk without Vows or Walls." *Merton Annual* 25 (2012) 154–68.

———. "Thomas Merton and St. John of the Cross: Lives on Fire." *Merton Annual* 21 (2008) 205–13.

Clarke, John, trans. *St. Thérèse of Lisieux: Her Last Conversations.* Washington, DC: Institute of Carmelite Studies, 1977.

Cunningham, Lawrence. *Thomas Merton. Spiritual Master: The Essential Writings.* Mahwah, NJ: Paulist, 1992.

Dashiff, Carol, et al. "Physician and Nurse Collaboration in a Medical Clinic for Indigent Patients." *Family Systems Medicine* 8 (1990) 57–70.

Dieker, Bernadette, and Jonathan Montaldo. *Merton and Hesychasm: The Eastern Church and the Prayer of the Heart.* Louisville: Fons Vitae, 2003.

Ferguson, Ronald. *Chasing the Wild Goose: The Story of the Iona Community.* Glasgow: Wild Goose, 2006.

Finley, James. *Merton's Palace of Nowhere.* Notre Dame: Ave Maria, 1978.

Foster, Richard. *Sanctuary of the Soul: Journey into Meditation.* Downers Grove: InterVarsity, 2011.

Francis. *Misericordiae Vultus: Bull of Indiction of the Extraordinary Jubilee of Mercy.* https://w2.vatican.va/content/francesco/en/apost_letters/documents/papa-francesco_bolla_20150411_misericordiae-vultus.html.

Goodloe, Nancy R., and Patricia M. Arreola. "Spiritual Health: Out of the Closet." *Journal of Health Education* 23 (1992) 221–226.

Greiner, Doris, and Nass Cannon. "I Sent Myself a Card Today." In *Caring: The Compassionate Healer*, edited by D. Gaut and M. Leininger, 115–121. New York: National League for Nursing, 1991.

Hart, Patrick. *A Monastic Vision for the Twenty-First Century.* Kalamazoo, MI: Cistercian, 2006.

John of the Cross, *The Complete Works of St. John of the Cross.* Edited by E. Allison Peers. Westminster, MD: Newman, 1964.

Joncas, Michael. "On Eagle's Wings." Recorded 1979 by North American Liturgy Resources.

Kohn, Alfie. "Caring Kids, the Role of the Schools." *Phi Delta Kappan* 72 (1991) 496–506.

Lewis, C. S. *A Grief Observed.* San Francisco: HarperOne, 2015.

Linn, Dennis, and Matthew Linn. *Healing Life's Hurts: Healing Memories through the Five Stages of Forgiveness.* New York: Paulist, 1972.

Luce, Clare Booth, ed. *Saints for Now.* New York: Sheed & Ward, 1952.

MacNutt, Francis. *The Power to Heal.* Notre Dame: Ave Maria, 1977.

Maher, Michael Forest, and Trina K. Hunt. "Spirituality Reconsidered." *Counseling and Values* 38 (1993) 21–28.

Manning, Doug. *Don't Take My Grief Away: What To Do When You Lose a Loved One.* San Francisco: Harper & Row, 1984.

Merton, Thomas. *The Ascent to Truth.* New York: Harcourt Brace, 1981.

———. *The Asian Journal of Thomas Merton.* New York: New Directions, 1975.

———. *Conjectures of a Guilty Bystander.* New York, Image Books, 1968.

———. *Contemplation in a World of Action.* New York: Doubleday, 1965.

———. *Contemplative Prayer.* New York: Image, 1971.

———. *Disputed Questions.* New York: Farrar, Straus, and Cudahy, 1960.

———. *Gandhi on Non-Violence.* New York: New Directions, 1964.

———. *The Hidden Ground of Love: Letters on Religious Experience and Social Concerns.* Edited by William H. Shannon. New York: Farrar, Straus and Giroux, 1985.

———. *Honorable Reader: Reflections on My Work.* Edited by Robert E. Daggy. New York: Crossroad, 1989.

———. *The Inner Experience: Notes on Contemplation.* Edited by William H. Shannon. San Francisco: Harper, 2003.

———. "A Letter to Pablo Antonia Cuadra Concerning Giants." In *The Collected Poems of Thomas Merton*, 384. New York: New Directions, 1977.

———. *Love and Living.* Edited by Naomi Burton Stone and Brother Patrick Hart. New York: Farrar, Straus and Giroux, 2011.

———. *The Monastic Journey.* New York: Image, 1974.

———. *Mystics and Zen Masters.* New York: Farrar, Straus and Giroux, 1967.

———. *The New Man.* New York: Fararr, Straus and Giroux, 2011.

———. *New Seeds of Contemplation.* New York: New Directions, 1972.

———. *No Man Is an Island.* New York: Harcourt Brace Jovanovich, 1955.

———. *The Road to Joy: Letters to Old and New Friends.* Edited by Robert E. Daggy. New York: Farrar, Straus and Giroux, 2011. eBook.

———. *The Seven Storey Mountain.* New York: Harcourt, Brace, 1948.

———. *The Sign of Jonas.* New York: Harcourt Brace Jovanovich, 1979.

———. *The Silent Life.* New York: Farrar, Straus and Giroux, 1957.

———. "The Stranger: Poverty of an Antihero." In *The Literary Essays of Thomas Merton*, 301. New York: New Directions, 1985.

———. *Thomas Merton: Essential Writings.* Edited by Christine M. Bochen. Maryknoll, NY: Orbis, 2000.

———. *Thomas Merton in Alaska: Prelude to the Asian Journal: The Alaskan Conferences, Journals, and Letters.* Edited by Robert E. Daggy. New York: New Directions, 1989.

———. *A Thomas Merton Reader.* Edited by Thomas P. McDonnell. New York: Image, 1974.

———. *The Wisdom of the Desert.* New York: New Directions, 1970.

———. *Zen and the Birds of Appetite.* New York: New Directions, 1968.

Mitsuda, Yasunori. "Small Two of Pieces." Track 19 on *Xenogears Original Soundtrack*, Japan, 1998.

Montaldo, Jonathan, and Gray Henry, eds. *Merton and Buddhism: Wisdom, Emptiness, and Everyday Mind.* Louisville: Fons Vitae, 2007.

Nouwen, Henri J. M. *The Wounded Healer: Ministry in Contemporary Society.* New York: Image, 1979.

Roach, M. Simone. *The Human Act of Caring: A Blueprint for the Health Professions.* Ottawa: Canadian Hospital Association, 1992.

Schofer, Peter. "The Rhetoric of the Text: Causality, Metaphor, and Irony." In *Camus's L'Etranger: Fifty Years On*, edited by Adele King, 139–51. New York: Springer, 1992.

Serafim, Sarovskiĭ. *St. Seraphim of Sarov Spiritual Instructions.* Translated by Seraphim Rose. Platina, CA: St. Herman of Alaska Brotherhood, 1996.

Starck, Patricia, and John P. McGovern, eds. *The Hidden Dimension of Illness: Human Suffering.* New York: National League for Nursing, 1992.

Teasdale, Wayne. *A Monk in the World.* Novato, CA: New World Library, 2003.

Bibliography

———. *The Mystic Heart: Discovering a Universal Spirituality in the World's Religions*. Novato, CA: New World Library, 1999.

Thayer-Bacon, Barbara J. "Caring and Its Relationship to Critical Thinking." *Educational Theory* 43 (1993) 323–40.

Tutu, Desmond Mpilo. *God Is Not a Christian and Other Provocations*. Edited by John Allen. New York: HarperOne, 2011.

Ward, Benedicta. *The Sayings of the Desert Fathers*. Oxford: A. R. Mowbray, 1975.

Wilson-Hartgrove, Jonathan. *New Monasticism*. Grand Rapids: Brazos, 2008.

Van Breemen, Peter. *As Bread That Is Broken*. Denville, NJ: Dimension, 1974.